A Woman's Path to Wholeness

The Gift Is In The Process

by

CAROLYN PORTER

"Carolyn's book touched, moved and inspired me to now live an empowered life. It made me want to generate new possibilities for my life that go beyond what my past beliefs say are possible, so that I can also be a winner!"
—GLORIA DORSEY-CHATHAM, Allen, Texas, *Singer*

"The message in this book comes from the soul of one who is living through this process called "life" and emerging victorious. The excitement is contagious and leapt off the pages, and by the end of the book I felt like soaring because I knew that I too can make a difference in this world."
—GLENDA LAWRENCE, Eads, Tennessee, *Music Instructor*

"Carolyn Porter leads us on her private journey through transformation of body, mind and spirit. Her courageous story sets the stage for unleashing the wisdom and joy possible for all who wish to meet life's challenges as opportunities from God. A must read for all women at a crossroad in their life, whether it be marriage or divorce."
—BARBARA LAMERDIN, Santa Fe, New Mexico, *Speaker and Consultant*

"As Carolyn journeys along her path to wholeness and takes us with her, we gain many pearls of wisdom. Her enlightenment will help others on their life's journey if they will take the time to stop, read, listen, ponder and learn."
—CHARLENE NELSON, Layton, Utah, *Executive*

To my precious children:
Stephen, Deborah, Scott, Melinda and Mande,
who are truly magnificent gifts from God!

Published by Empower Productions
205 Ridgepoint Court
Woodstock, GA 30188

First printing May 2001

Library of Congress: 2001090586

ISBN: 0-9711150-0-1

Printed by Transcontinental Printing
100 Jameson Drive
Peterborough, Ontario K9J 6X6
e.mail address: bestbook@sympatico.ca

Cover design by Paula Chance
Book design by Jill Dible
Edited by Dorian Gibson and Mary Dumark

ACKNOWLEDGEMENTS

To my cherished mentor, Dr. Michael J. Duckett, whose powerful influence helped transform my life and who has continually encouraged me, thus propelling me towards my potential.

To my loving friend, Deanna, who blesses my life and has always been there for me no matter what.

To my Dad, Mom, John, Beverly, and all other family members who have participated in my life.

To Thea, Beverly and Raquel, whose inspiration in one way or another has directly contributed to this writing.

To Dorian and Mary, who edited this book - a job so worthy of acknowledgement.

To all those whose footprints are forever embedded in my heart.

CONTENTS

COMES THE DAWN

After a while you learn the subtle difference
Between holding a hand and chaining a soul,
And you learn that love doesn't mean leaning
And company doesn't mean security,
And you begin to understand that kisses aren't contracts
And presents aren't promises,
And you begin to accept your defeats
With your head held high and your eyes open,
With the grace of a woman, not the grief of a child.
You learn to build your roads
On today because tomorrow's ground
Is too uncertain for plans, and futures have
A way of falling down in mid-flight.
After a while you learn that even sunshine
Burns if you get too much,
So you plant your own garden and decorate
Your own soul, instead of waiting
For someone to bring you flowers.
And you learn that you really can endure,
That you really are strong
And you really do have worth,
And you learn and learn. . . and you learn
With every goodbye you learn.

—AUTHOR UNKNOWN

INTRODUCTION

❧

I share my story with you for one reason and one reason only - to help you understand how far off you can be and yet come about face and get it all straight. No matter where you are in your life you can change your course; it is all up to you! So many women go through life taking care of everyone else and forgetting they are individuals who have a lot to offer, and have a life purpose of their own; in fact this is the real reason we are here. A female is basically brought up to believe that she must get married, take care of her husband, meet his needs, take care of the children and their activities, cook, clean etc., and some do this in addition to a job outside the home. But where is her soul? What about her inner self? What would happen to her if her family and her job dropped off the face of the earth; where would she be? Would she fold up and say what's the use of living now? Would she pick up the pieces little by little until she found someone else to take care of and/or a new job? Or would she proceed with her purpose in life, which involves loving, giving and serving with no thought of what she'll get out of it? Very few women fall into the last category but that's where we should all be. Look at women who lose a mate through death or divorce. Many flounder around for years or forever, bemoaning their miserable fate, and fail to see their worth and potential. Most wish for another relationship to fill their own void of not knowing who they are, the purpose of their life on this planet. Some hurry into another relationship only to find themselves right back where they were before - depending on someone else for their value and happiness, which of course can never happen. I was no different from any of you; I thought the same way. But one by one things began to occur that opened my eyes to the void in my life, and none of them were coincidences. God knows exactly what we need exactly at the time we need it and His timing is always perfect. I used to say, look at all those wasted years and why did it have to take so long? None were wasted! There is a reason for everything and His answers come in His time, not ours.

The year 2000 has ushered in an age of women taking the lead. Love, caring and compassion are beginning to dominate, and it's about time. We're in an age of spirituality, not just religion, and I hope I can show you how each one of us has the qualities of loving and serving and has a unique and wonderful communion with God available to us at all times. But it requires giving up our control in trying to figure out our lives and letting Him work out the details. Surrender is the hardest lesson most will ever have to learn. It certainly was mine. It's a process that makes us continually turn our lives over and we never stop working on it.

As my story unfolds, you will most likely see parts of your own life in mine, feelings that are shared, problems as well as joys. This is because we are actually all one, having been created by God. We are all part of each other. So being part of God we share a great deal. The scenario may be different for each one of us, but as I hear stories from other people I realize the thoughts, feelings and patterns are often the same. It doesn't matter what your circumstances or your perceptions are at this moment, because you can change both of these if you choose to. Our minds control our thoughts and our thoughts create our lives through the words we speak and the actions we take. Stop and think a minute about your mind and its power. You recall a painful experience at the dentist so, in anticipation of the next trip, you get nervous about going. Perhaps you're afraid to fly in an airplane so as your scheduled trip approaches, you get diarrhea. This is called fear, an imaginary thought created in your mind of something not even real. No one can think in your mind but you, so you have to take all the responsibility for your life as it is: you are exactly where you expect yourself to be. If you don't like where you are, change it, create a new picture. As you think, so it is! Life is meant to be enjoyed in peacefulness and happiness when it's turned over to God and we can just be. I love the phrase, let go and let God; it's the only way. As I unfold my story I pray God will open your hearts, for it all begins in the heart. This is where you realize that no matter what point you are in your life, it's never too late to change your life into what you want it to be, and make it a celebration!

PART I

My Story

A new life begins
how to unfold,
'tis a mystery only time reveals.

— CAROLYN PORTER

CHAPTER 1

❧

In the Beginning

I don't remember my birth although I've been told it almost happened in the car on the way to the hospital. My dad was away in the war so my uncle had to take my mom to the hospital. Can't you just imagine what was going through his mind? Sheer panic! I believe I was in a hurry to make my entrance and get this show on the road because, for a first birth, it was supposed to take much longer than it did.

As I grew I turned out to be a shy child, but wait until I got to know you! When I was four years old my grandparents took me on a train trip so that I could experience another facet of life, being that I lived in a small town in Southern New Jersey. I got bored because they were sleeping so I began investigating all the neat buttons on the seats. To my childish delight I pushed a couple of buttons that caused some activity. These buttons released the reclining seats and flipped my grandparents into an upright position, jarring them from their peaceful slumber. Although peals of laughter echoed through the train, I was scolded and dutifully put back in my seat. These situations seemed to become regular occurrences throughout my childhood. Although I was basically a good child, I didn't like so many restrictions and longed for more activity.

࿇

My parents were ultra religious and we attended church on Sunday morning and Sunday night, Wednesday and Friday evenings. There were devotions every morning and/or evening and Sunday afternoon was devoted to napping or playing Bible games. After I ate breakfast I didn't want to sit in my chair to have devotions, I wanted to get outside and play. I could hear the kids out there playing and believe me I can't remember a single thing from those devotions.

When I was nine my mom decided it was time I learned about the birds and the bees. We had a separate garage behind our house and I was allowed to play in there and had part of it set up as a pretend house with my dolls, etc. My best friend was the guy next door, and although I played tag football with him and all the guys in the neighborhood, I often had him play "house" with me. I don't think the poor guy really wanted to play house so much but he would acquiesce. (I think that's called sharing, or is it controlling?) On this particular day I decided it was time to tell him where babies come from and also about a girls "monthly", now that I was so grown-up and knew so much about these things. You should have seen the look on his face as I unfolded the details: basically terror, then relief when he realized he wasn't a girl! Of course, the next day his mom came over in a major huff and was very upset with me for telling him this information. I thought it was funny because he was such a mama's boy and needed to know these things.

We had love in our house and family, but it was a stern, formal love with only traditional goodbye or goodnight hugs or a kiss. I always felt I had to toe the line or be punished, that's what God's word said. When I didn't toe the line I'd have to stand in the corner, write sentences about how I wanted to be better, endure a belt making contact with my backside, or those horrible times when I told a lie or talked back and had soap scrubbed

❧

into my gagging mouth! Somehow though, I kept repeating actions that brought me the same consequences. I vowed I would never, I repeat NEVER, punish my own children with any of these things when I had some of my own one day. Guess what? I gave them the same punishments! Thankfully though, I only used this approach in the early years of motherhood.

It was decided that I should take piano lessons when I was nine. I loved it for the first three months and then I hated it, but was made to continue. One day I was so mad when I couldn't play something correctly that I slammed my fist down on the keyboard, only to feel the piano bench start falling due to my exertion. To my utter dismay the leg broke as the bench toppled to the floor. Of course I had to pay for the repair and with an allowance of only $.25 per week it took quite a while to complete. Did that teach me patience and obedience? Of course not! Later on, however, after many years of piano lessons, I became a rather accomplished pianist and operated my own piano studio for 32 years. Do parents really know best?

At age nine I became the proud sister to a baby brother and became his little mother. Finally there was another child to share my life with. I knew then I wanted to have lots of children and I achieved that desire later in my life. As my brother grew I took him everywhere and loved it. At 13 a baby sister came into my life and I was ecstatic. Although I still loved taking care of my brother there was now a baby to whom I could be a mother. I had begun to improve my sewing skills, having taken a class in seventh grade. I began making clothes for her in her toddler years. At 17 I even took her to college classes with me a couple different days - I had graduated early from high school due, I was told, to my brains. She would sit quietly and color or draw and I thought it fun. Becoming a mother was definitely on my agenda.

*The most amazing view the bird sees
is when it leaves the nest
and tries its wings for the first time.*

—Carolyn Porter

❧

CHAPTER 2

Growing Up

As the teen years progressed and the novelty of being a "mother" wore off, it was replaced with an unbelievable interest in male friends and the so-called "rebellious" era of my life ensued. I seemed to be sent to my room a lot or slapped across the face because I couldn't seem to say the correct things. If I lied I got in trouble or if I told the truth I'd be punished for the "bad" thing I had done or said. I mentioned earlier that I had to go to church on Friday nights. There we had lessons and recited catechism verses and then played ping-pong. I hated ping-pong unless there were some neat guys there, which rarely happened. I wanted to dance but it wasn't allowed in our church and I never understood that, because the Bible is loaded with references to dancing and praising God. Anyhow, I learned of a block party through one of the girls in the church that was being held a few blocks from the church one Friday night. The pastor always left during "social hour" and would come back at the end, so I herded most of the kids to the block party, planning to be back before the pastor came back. We all had a great time dancing, eating and having fun. I was dancing away when suddenly a firm hand grabbed the back of my neck and abruptly ushered me away from my partner into his car with the other kids from church.

❦

The pastor had of course come back early that night and one of the kids who had stayed behind informed him of our "sinful" departure. We were then taken to the pastor's study at his home and he began praying with us. He had called all the parents and informed them that we couldn't leave until we all confessed our sin and apologized for it. One by one everyone began to apologize, except me. I wasn't sorry so why should I lie and apologize? Finally, after an hour or so and some not so-kindly-looks from my fellow sinners, I decided it wasn't fair to keep every one there because of me, so I apologized, keeping my fingers crossed of course. When my dad picked me up he mentioned he was glad I finally saw the error in my ways and had apologized. I informed him that I wasn't sorry at all but had only apologized because I didn't want everyone else to suffer on my account. My openess shocked my serious-minded dad who promptly punished me for not only leaving church, but for lying. I just figured "dammed if I do and dammed if I don't." But I got him back a few weeks later when, at 14, I was French-kissed for the first time by my boyfriend in the back seat while my dad was driving us home, and he didn't even know! Parents are so blind sometimes!

I was sent to a Christian high school that was a good ways from my home; it involved a four-hour treck of train and bus to and from school every day, and I had to do this for four years. Needless to say, I stayed with friends who lived near school as often as I could, especially since I played basketball and field hockey. One girl I especially liked. She had a "neat" family because we could do things that I wasn't allowed to do, so I stayed with her the most. As often as possible, she and I would invite boys over, at least five, to play spin the bottle (I mean study) in her recreational room. Get those odds - two girls and five or more guys! We would have contests to see which "couple" could kiss the longest and I usually won. So much for studying.

❧

Before you get an unclear picture of me, I really was a pretty good kid; I was just high-spirited and at the same time stifled. I liked to have fun and do "fun things," but my interpretation of "fun things" didn't exactly fit with my parents' interpretation. This is often the case! I resented spending so much sacred time in church. I resented the control of my life as I was expanding and experiencing my teenage years. All those rules! I'm not saying I was right and they were wrong, for each person has to decide that for themselves, but I do know now that you can never make anyone do what you want, think the way you think, or act the way you do, no matter how much you try to control them. All you can do is be a guide and maybe use a little gentle persuasion at times.

I began my early motherhood years as a disciplinarian, using control in many ways. Later I realized you can't control another person no matter how many rules or how much punishment you inflict; it sure doesn't work with someone who is high-spirited! I now feel that showing warm love rather than fear is the way to get the best response— the response you desire. There must be some restrictions of course. After all, that shows those dear teenagers we love them, but we must remember they are growing too and have to learn much through their own experiences, within reason.

I was a person who became nervous easily. In sixth grade I played the piano for Sunday School and I remember being so nervous - sweaty palms, heart racing, trembling knees. I played my first piano solo for my eighth grade graduation and was shaking all over, but I did a great job with no audible mistakes. To show you just how nervous I would get, let me share this episode with you. In tenth grade my parents decided I needed to enter the spring contest of art, drama and music at our school. If you won you went on to compete with district

❧

Christian schools. There was a girl in eleventh grade who played beautifully I thought, so I didn't want to enter and compete against her and lose. My parents entered me anyhow and I was having fits because I *really* did not want to do this. I mean I might make a fool out of myself, right? But I had no way out, or wait a minute, maybe there was a way out. I decided to hammer my finger, (yes, I really took a hammer and beat my finger to death) until the pain was too great, hoping I would break it or at least sprain it. That's how much I did not want to enter that contest! My finger swelled up and turned purple, green and blue and I thought all was safe now. But I forgot one thing, actually two things, God was in control and my dad had a Ph.D. in Pharmacology. When he saw my finger he promptly made up some soaking concoctions and, voila, my finger improved just in time to perform. Incidentally, I told my dad I had injured my finger in a door. With trembling knees and sweaty palms I played my solo and to my utter amazement I won the contest. You see, the eleventh grader who I thought played so well, had very poor rhythm and judges don't like that. I had received a near-perfect score. What a day! My life began a new turn with some confidence forming, and when I won the district, wow, things sure seemed rosier. It's amazing how one event can make such a change in one's life. What I saw much later in life was that the fear of not performing perfectly was a negative emotion always underlying my life.

College brought new dilemmas and new challenges. I found going to a large, non-sheltered, secular university quite difficult at first - so many people, so much "worldliness" and so much about life of which I knew little. I was in the music department which, being a much smaller group than the entire student body, offered me some security, a safe haven from so many new people. Here was my chance for lots of freedom, but having never had it

⤎⤏

and maybe suffering the fear of being punished if I took advantage of it, I developed a spastic colon, which is a stress reaction. I was not allowed to study on Sunday but, with taking the fullest load of college courses and both teaching piano and working at a nearby Kroger, I found it difficult not to study on Sunday. At final exam time in my sophomore year of college, I announced I wouldn't be going to church that particular Sunday night due to three exams the next day that I needed to prepare for. It didn't go over too well and I was told to go to church and that if I didn't, because of other disobediences that I had accumulated, I would have to move out and find my own place to live. Needless to say, I went to a friend's house and studied until 2 a.m. and did well on my exams. On Thursday evening, after the completion of all my exams, my dad informed me I needed to find a place to live. The next day I found an apartment and moved out a few days later into a different world - independence, or was it?

Now I could do what I wanted - have parties, stay out to 4 a.m., drink, dance, anything I wanted to - I'll never tell which, if any, I did! I got to work more hours, pay all my own bills, buy my own clothes, my own food, clean and cook in addition to study and it was all such fun. How could my dad have done this to me - such responsibility at just barely 19? I'm sure he did this out of love as well as because of my disobediences, but it was definitely the best thing that had happened to me up to then.

I worked hard as this was my nature. When I had a task to complete I always finished it and did it well. This was a challenge that I met head on. I paid my bills and even had money left over, and eventually bought my own piano so that I didn't have to use my parent's piano for all the piano lessons I was then teaching. I had a roommate twice, but neither wanted to do her part with either cleaning or paying the bills, so I decided I liked it better by myself. I had a steady boyfriend who later would become my husband, and it got complicated when both my roommate and I wanted to entertain or cook for our boyfriend at the same time. Holding two jobs, a full load of classes, university chorus accompanist, piano lessons of my own and my own place to keep up kept me busy. I'm not deserving a pat on the back for meeting this challenge, because I know so many people who had a much more difficult challenge than this, but I do thank God I had this challenge. Was this merely coincidence? There is no such thing!

Sweet child, thou didst come from heaven to me
on loan from the Father above,
I gently do guide, have so many dreams,
your own mind you use, so I just love.

What joy you have brought along with the tears
so swiftly the years do roll by,
for now it is time that you try your own wings
and find how to live your own life.

The memories so sweet deeply etched in my heart
are treasures God gave don't you see,
your feet find their own path as I give you back
to the Father who loaned you to me.

—CAROLYN PORTER

❧

CHAPTER 3

Caretaking

I was in love! It wasn't the first time but this was special. Remember that? There are no words to describe all those warm feelings and there are flowers and gifts and day-dreaming and long walks and talks, and you're with him all the time, sharing and caring and then it's decision time - either we break up or get married because there is no other place to go. All my friends were married by then; I'd been in all their weddings as a bridesmaid, so marriage seemed logical. We both agreed. So at 22 I tied the knot before I got too old! I even made my own wedding gown - remember my sewing. We had a big splash on Thanksgiving night. Then the bliss began, or so I thought.

Marriage is always a big adjustment for each person, but for some it's harder than others. Ours was middle of the road, after all, we had been dating for three and a half years. But it wasn't long until irritations began to surface and explosions ripped through the rooms, remembering, of course, my quiet, shy nature. We managed to make it through these minor adjustments and the first pregnancy occurred. Obviously it was not in God's plan because it ended in a miscarriage 10 weeks later. I was devastated; after all I had been waiting a lot of years to start those babies. Time kept marching on and no further pregnancy and I

❧

became very melancholy. There were tests and more tests but all to no avail. I actually told my husband that if I couldn't have babies I didn't want to live. Can you imagine how that must have made him feel? Was there something wrong with that mindset? In God's timing a pregnancy happened and this time all went well; once I got started there was no stopping me. I birthed five living children, two sons and three daughters, having one other miscarriage before number four. I loved being pregnant, after the third month that is, and was proud of all that it meant. Childbirth was easy and fast for me, even though I was and am a size two and had several nine-pound babies. Motherhood suited me well and I gave a lot to my children; it was all I had dreamed it would be and more.

By the time the third child was born there were many problems developing in the marriage. I felt I had so much of the responsibility and was teaching 30 or so piano students every week as well. I was a good cook and seamstress and created many of my children's clothes as well as my own; I was always cooking and entertaining. I even undertook craft-making and sold things in shows and shops. But where was my help? He was often in front of the TV. Resentment set in.

It was time for counseling but that didn't work either. However, we kept trying— mainly covering up and pretending. It was like living on the proverbial roller-coaster, up and down, up and down. Later that roller-coaster couldn't get to the top. Children four and five came into existence and talk about responsibility and busy! I was up to 45 students per week and had become a church pianist and a music arranger on the side. I was too busy to worry too much about the marriage. I was unhappy and he was too, but we kept trying, or so we thought. Something inside of me kept saying, isn't there more than this? But, as the religious teachings stated, there was no way out without adultery.

Before I go any further, I have to say that I believe in the sanctity of marriage and I believe far too many people give up without trying hard enough, but I no longer feel people should stay together if they are not nurturing each other and helping each other to grow. If there is a great deal of anger, coldness, unhappiness and verbal or mental abuse, what kind of a life is that for the children? Do you think you can hide it from them, or is it fair for them to live in an unloving, unhappy environment? They get the wrong picture about how marriage should be.

Don't get me wrong, there were a lot of fun times, especially with five kids, but what was missing, I later discovered, was the spiritual connection, the sharing of the souls and the companionship that, in my opinion, is an absolutely positive necessity for a good and lasting partnership. Romance is programmed into us in a misguided way through the media, TV and movies, etc. Love and subsequently marriage are warm loving feelings, dreaming about each other, staring into each others eyes, candlelight dinners, gifts, flowers, doing special things for the other and sharing common interests. That's all great, nice and important, but it's not real, genuine love. On the contrary, it's passion, infatuation, hormones, puppy love or whatever you want to call it, but it's not real, true love. Real love is spiritual first, a companionship and deep friendship that grows and grows. It allows the people involved to "pierce the armor that hides their hearts; the heart breaks and then it soars" as Marianne Williamson writes in *Enchanted Love*. This is real love that lasts and, upon analyzing the divorce rate, you can judge for yourself how many couples have real love. Then how many experience lonely, unhappy lives within their marriage, but are afraid to leave. Most people start with the physical and never reach the spiritual.

All during these child-rearing years I experienced many joys - being a mother was a dream come true. I ate it up! Although I might complain about all there was to do at times and was often tired, I really put a lot of time into mothering. I pushed myself to do many other things, and I seemed to need to hear some praise for my accomplishments. I always loved it when people said I did enough for three people, or if you want something done ask Carolyn to do it and it'll get done. I had added chairman and vice-president of music organizations and social chairman of adults at church to my list of activities. I was always into something new, needing another lift. It wasn't that my husband didn't praise me because he frequently did, but there was always the underlying disconnection with little communication. We didn't share common interests and there was no spiritual connection.

I had developed many physical maladies over the years and although none serious, they kept me from operating at peak and enjoying life totally. The spastic colon continually surfaced as well as headaches, sinus congestion, low-back pain and sciatica, TMJ, and never-ending insomnia. I used tranquilizers, analgesics, and decongestants, but as the years rolled by I knew I had to find alternative ways to deal with these problems and not take drugs. They were not a cure, only a bandage. Of course the underlying stress was the reason for all of these problems, as I discovered later, but how could I avoid that? Other people had worse problems than I did and didn't seem to have these physical disorders. Why me? Little did I know all that was in store for me, for you see, God was about to start a series of events that would continue in the years ahead. There was work for me to do (oh great, more work!) and lessons to be learned.

All of my life I have been a busy person, not still very much, not taking time to know who I am, but being a caretaker. It seemed like that was what I was supposed to do. After all, weren't women taught at that time to get married, have kids, take care of them and their husbands and their homes? That's what I did. I loved being a mom; remember I had been dreaming of babies for years. I sewed clothes for all of us and was always baking something special, cooking fancy meals and doing the housewife routine. Most of all I loved having neighborhood kids over at our house. They so appreciated the extras I did for my own kids because their moms didn't do any of it. We moved a lot with my husband's job and each time we moved we would get a bigger house, putting much of our money into the house. I always wanted something special to draw friends to our house, so we had basements with recreational rooms and even a ping-pong table, swimming pools, volleyball and in one place two German Shepherds that I bred and sold their puppies. There were always kittens around because of the cats I had. But I didn't stop there. I taught piano students, 30 to 45 per week and often hosted local competitions. I also accompanied choirs and soloists and for three years was a church pianist. I was an officer in various music organizations. Many times I arranged music for my students and eventually had three pieces copyrighted. Then of course there were sports events, church activities and many other functions. I didn't believe in paying for anything that I could do myself (could that be my conservative upbringing?) so I wallpapered and stenciled walls and sewed drapes and made every kind of home decoration imaginable. I even upholstered a sofa and chair once. What a life! I was always busy and could accomplish a lot, all in the name of love and devotion and maybe a little neediness for praise. The more you love your family the more you serve them, right? Believe me, serving your family is admirable and people praised me all the time for my accomplishments, but where was I? My marriage was unhappy so I made my children my happiness and gleaned all kinds of love, support and fulfillment for my neediness from them. After all, I was the caretaker - they depended on me and I was always there. But I had become lost in the

⤎

years of motherhood and enduring physical ailments that I drowned with tranquilizers. I never could understand why I had so many minor ailments, so I blamed it on my failing marriage, stress, finances and stuffed it all back inside and kept going. Sound familiar? What else could I do with it?

My kids and I were always creating something like a playhouse, tree swings, forts in the woods, skateboard ramps; I enjoyed creating things and joining in with the kids. Dad helped too at times. Several of my kids are creative, one son in particular, and made fantastic Halloween yard displays including a full-sized coffin complete with skeleton, gravestones and all the trimmings. Some kids were too afraid to come to our door because it was so realistic! I always decorated big time at holidays and they would help; it was fun. When they had bicycles I got one and rode with them. When roller blades were in I got a pair and acquired a much lesser skill than they. I did draw the line at skateboarding.

Probably the most relaxed and fun place we lived was in Tallahassee, Florida. We had two acres in a rural area, a 42 foot swimming pool complete with palm trees I had hauled in, a dirt volley ball court and the two German Shepherds. Our house was headquarters and I had so many parties because there was always something to do at our house. I also organized a homeowners' association. But my gardens were my pride and joy. I grew everything from vegetables to peanuts, watermelons and fruit trees. I rarely had to buy vegetables and never potatoes or onions. I could work my tiller like any man! I had cut my piano students down to 14 or 15 per week because I was burning out from teaching.

Guess what happened. My children were growing up. You wake up one day to the realization that these precious spirits who are part of you are beginning to leave - these gifts from God who were on loan to you for a few short years are about to find their own place in the world- and mom isn't needed in the same way. A great emptiness begins to creep into your soul, but then you realize this is the natural progression of life, a transition necessary for growth, for both mom and the children. But the pain can be excruciating, especially if you feel that once your children are gone there's not much else after that. Can you imagine that thought pattern? I was there, after all, my children were my life. This is exactly what happens to many women, even if it's subconscious. Wake up! There's a wonderful life out there, to be you, to love, to serve and share your many other gifts to the world. Now it's time for you and your purpose to unfold and know what your soul has to give.

The oldest son had left for college but came home every few weekends, so that wasn't too bad. Besides, I still had four left to keep me busy. But something else happened while we were there. My oldest daughter caught the love bug and it looked like a wedding would be happening. So now what, one in college and a wedding; that meant money. There was one problem - we kept putting the money into bigger houses and extras and there wasn't much left to work with. That didn't stop me; in fact, it became my ultimate challenge. Those creative skills like sewing and decorating were about to be put to the test. The wedding was scheduled for spring, so that gave me six and a half months. My daughter wanted me to make her gown and we decided I would create all the bouquets, corsages, boutonnieres, church floral sprays, reception table centerpieces, topiary trees, bows etc., and even all the floral decorations for the cake. They would be silk flowers.

A sparkling vision in white,
a young girl's dream;
misty eyes, in love her hand is given,
glowing candles dance as two hearts unite.
'Tis a day for enchanting memories.

—CAROLYN PORTER

❧

CHAPTER 4

The Big Event

As I began to envision the wedding in my mind I realized the first step was to get a decorator's license for $15. No problem, now I was a decorator. The next thing was my daughter's gown and that was the biggest challenge. It was to be a formal evening wedding and we picked three patterns that I would use parts of to give her the look she wanted. It was yards and yards of fabric, almost daily laborious work, and the finished product included much of my own design with the hand-sewing of 35,000 pearls and sequins. It took two and a half months to complete. Of course I got everything discounted because of my decorator's license.

She had decided on 10 bridesmaids and I was to make seven of those gowns, my gown, the flower girl's gown, not to mention the matching outfits that I made for my three daughters and myself for the rehearsal dinner. Then there were the flowers. I ordered everything from Atlanta and turned a small room into a florist shop. It was a great deal of fun for me. I love to create things and watch them come together. I did some elaborate arrangements and well over a 100 bouquets and corsages. I hired two friends to help prepare the food. They smoked the turkeys and hams and gathered the fruit and veggies together. I made the mints, punch and mini dinner rolls. In fact, the day before the

❧

wedding I had uncles, aunts, brother, sister, cousins, grandparents and anyone else I could grab, rolling dough for those mini dinner rolls. You should have seen them, flour on their faces and clothes and the shapes of some of those rolls! They all sat outside on the deck by the pool and it was a sight to behold. I'm sure all those men were glad when that task was accomplished.

I had been able to purchase everything (cake knife, bride book, etc.) at a lesser price and had shopped around for the best cake and photographer price I could find but still with a good reputation. I rented a limousine, a disc jockey and three TV cameras for the video. Everything was ready. Relatives from several states were there and they pitched in the day of the wedding to help. We were at the church at nine a.m. to decorate while the bridesmaids and bride got their hair done. One-thirty took us to the reception location to complete decorating with balloons, flowers and all the trimmings. I got home at 4:15 and was to be picked up by the limo at 5:00 p.m. I have never moved faster in my life! I was supposed to have been home at 3:00 p.m. for a leisurely preparation time! It went off without a hitch, almost. One boutonniere was misplaced so I had to take a flower out of a couple bouquets and improvise a boutonniere. Then the flower girl decided to walk on the lower layer of her dress rather than the steps, subsequently tearing a whole section of the dress out from the seam. Fortunately I had thought ahead and whipped out my emergency kit and promptly hand-sewed the dress back in place moments before the entrance music began. As I saw it unfold before my eyes I was proud of what I had accomplished. Everyone called me a multi-talented super-mom, but all I could think of was my daughter, who had gone through some rough times and I felt she deserved this day of being a queen. I had done it all for only $6,200! I didn't realize the appreciation my daughter felt for me and what I had done for her until, in the middle of the ceremony, the pastor called me up onto the already packed platform and my daughter presented to me a plaque with a poem that said: To Mom With Love, and publicly thanked me. I almost lost it and the cameras picked that up on the video. I could hardly get down the steps for all the tears. Later she gave me a ring with a black onyx stone to remind me of the work I did. I still wear the ring and the plaque hangs on my wall. Was it worth all the long hours I spent in preparation? Absolutely! There are no words that could express the feelings I had as I stood on that platform and the thankfulness I felt having given of myself to her, in love. I have always viewed this as one of my biggest achievements in the first half of my life.

Time moved ahead; there was the arrival of two grandsons whom I watched make their entrance into the world and held screaming within moments of their birth. Then it was time to move back to Atlanta, business of course. This, our eighth move, would be different; I had to leave a child and two grandsons behind. Now I was beginning to see that these five precious loans I would have to give up one by one. It made me think, what happens when they are all gone? What kind of life will that be? - no children to take care of, no busyness to occupy my day. Oh, but wait a minute, isn't that when mom and dad do things and enjoy themselves, except this mom and dad couldn't do that. I had burned out of piano teaching but had been doing interior decorating for the last one and a half years. That's what I'd do, decorate homes and businesses. Actually it had all fallen into my lap, or was this God's plan? I had decided to decorate weddings but instead I was asked to decorate a couple of businesses and a complete house from the ground up. That sounded like fun. I had an eye for color and coordination, so why not. One of the businesses, though, was a mess. It would require hiring contractors to take out walls, hiring drywall specialists, painters, wallpaper hangers, none of which I had ever done before. Oh well, why not. So I did it and it looked great when it was completed - three offices and a reception area with new color schemes, drapes, flooring, wall decors, chairs, desks, the works. Now on to the house.

It was work, but fun. I helped pick almost everything in the decorating of the house. My husband and I hung the drapes I had designed and made for the house three days before we moved back to Atlanta. Kind of close, to be sure, but I made it.

Each moment of each day
the shadow of our footprints behind us stay;
our steps may falter and darkness blanket the path,
but heaven watches and lights the way.
Walking beside us, silently near,
encircling with love.
Gently, ever so gently, lifted up by angels' wings.

—CAROLYN PORTER

CHAPTER 5

✌

The Physical Realm

Just a few months before this move, in the middle of working on the house I was decorating, I had begun having symptoms that indicated stress overload. That was only part of it, because I later found out I also had a hormone imbalance at that time in a woman's life when change is imminent. Before I elaborate on the events surrounding this discovery, let me back up to a time about six years prior to that when myriads of symptoms were occurring and doctors kept giving me drugs which I didn't want to take anymore. The drugs didn't solve my problems, so I began to look for alternative reasons for these symptoms. Since I was taking my two youngest daughters to the library every week I started investigating subjects relating to nutrition and allergies. Every week I'd check books out and read different topics on health, and one time I found a book called *The Yeast Connection* by William C. Crook in the nutrition section by mistake. What a coincidence! When I looked on the cover every symptom I'd ever had since college was listed there. This book said I had candida, an excess of yeast in the body caused by antibiotics, stress and too much sugar. I had always been a sugarholic- remember all the baking I had done and still did? To cure it I had to cut out of my diet all sugar, yeast and dairy products in order to starve the yeast. That meant no

༕

desserts, cheese or bread, everything I loved. I thought I was so lucky because I could eat all those things and stay a size two or four, even after having five children. I shook and trembled, had a major headache and couldn't sleep much for the first five days, and it took three weeks to begin to feel normal again. I could only eat meat, veggies and a little fruit; my family didn't understand. They thought I was losing it. Maybe I was; I sure felt like I was. I figured that in a few months I could start to eat some of those wonderful foods again, but then I found out that since I had had this candida for so long it had become systemic, which meant it was all through my body and would be hard to eradicate. I had initially gone down to 98 pounds, 14 pounds below my usual weight. I had to cook my food separately and when we had parties I had to give up everything I loved. I couldn't even eat my homemade rolls that I was known for. I gradually gained my weight back and then I discovered a new challenge - how to make decent-tasting treats not using sugar. I learned to combine fruits for sweeteners, substituted rice milk for regular milk and studied and studied alternative health to continue improving my health. It was trial and error in my culinary creations, but I kept going until I had a few good-tasting things to eat. As I researched I discovered how bad white sugar, white flour and dairy are for human consumption and changed my attitude into being grateful that I had been given this health challenge. To this day, I never use dairy of any kind, rarely use unbleached white flour and replace sugar with raw honey or fruit. I have created some rather tasty recipes and find I no longer desire the sweets or processed food. I eat a lot of vegetables, many raw, and have learned much about achieving good health, which takes me to my next phase. Wasn't it amazing what one out-of-place book did? Not a coincidence!

Now back to six years later. In 1994 I went to a homeopathic (alternative) doctor a few months before our move to Atlanta, and he felt my symptoms were stress-related. He gave me what he thought was the appropriate dose of a homeopathic remedy that I later found out was the deepest-acting remedy for suppressed emotions. Within 24 hours of taking that one dose every anxious symptom I had ever experienced surfaced and I was a basket case. It was literally like having a nervous breakdown in one day. You see, homeopathy works by sometimes bringing a symptom to the surface so that you can get rid of it and be healed. I paced continuously, my insides shook, I could hardly eat and I would sleep two or three hours a night if I was lucky. My pulse rate stayed near 108, which was too high. The doctor had never had anyone react this way so he kept in daily contact with me. He said to hang in there and the symptoms would eventually go away, but after nine days of this I couldn't take it any longer and called an allopathic medical doctor and received a prescription of an anti-anxiety drug called Xanax. It gave immediate relief. I had been such a mess for those nine days that I couldn't even drive my van to pick up my daughters from school. Two months later I decided to get off of the Xanax because it is habit forming and I had learned of herbal substitutes that I wanted to try. The first few weeks were okay but then the symptoms began surfacing again. You see, the Xanax hadn't fixed anything, it only suppressed the symptoms, so they just resurfaced. In the meantime, my oldest son, who had switched from studying business to a chiropractic college in Atlanta and was studying nutrition, had suggested that he and I open a health store after I moved to Atlanta. He said because I now had a lot of knowledge about alternative medicine and because he was learning so much on the subject that we could do it. It sounded okay but I really wanted to decorate homes. As time went on, though, I decided the health store might be good. But how could I open a store feeling like I did? Besides, that meant going to

ℭ

work every day and I wasn't sure I wanted to do that or would be able to do it. He was so excited about the possibility and never quit talking about it. He would call every few days asking if I had thought any more about it. Finally, I said okay, let's check into it after I move to Atlanta.

I was back on Xanax because the symptoms were severe again. Little did I know I'd spend the next five years of my life peeling away layer after layer of suppressed emotional hurts and issues that had physically manifested themselves. The move was difficult even with the Xanax, and every month or so I'd "crack" again. I couldn't even stand to drive my van and be confined in such a small space. I immediately sought out natural health care doctors in Atlanta where, fortunately, there were many from which I could choose. I went from doctor to doctor trying all kinds of different things, but couldn't get well. Sometimes I'd feel so bad and so weak I'd just lie down on the floor right where I was and rest for 15 minutes or so before I could get up. I spent thousands of dollars on nutritional supplements, tests of every description, until finally we discovered that my adrenals were shot and that I was in peri-menopause. Of course my immune system was depressed also. One chiropractor/kinesiologist whom I frequented for a year and a half helped me in some ways, but seemed to keep my system in turmoil when constantly giving me homeopathic medicine. I didn't know better and kept taking them, until one day something inside me said this was not going to work and I quit taking them all. Later I discovered I am a very high-vibrational person and just can't take homeopathic treatment without reactions. I had even been using natural progesterone, so my hormones were better, but still needed help.

All through this weakness I couldn't stand being still. I pushed myself to continually do things. We had built a house bigger than the last one, of course. It was beautiful, on a lake, three stories with nearly 6,000 square feet of living area. I decorated it extensively but within a budget, hanging all the wallpaper myself, sewing all the window treatments, even to hand rubbing gold gild into wooden rods to make them look expensive. I thought to myself that it didn't matter how anxious I was or how much I was shaking because I was at home and could handle things better that way. Of course, none of this helped repair my adrenals but I knew of no other way to exist, except to keep moving and pushing to create, therefore feeling I was accomplishing something. It was the only way I knew to deal with my situation - keep moving - but I really wasn't dealing with anything; I just didn't want to think.

During all this sickness I felt very alone; sometimes I wondered if God had forgotten me. Would I ever be normal again? Would I make it? I tried reading many religious books including my Bible, but I was still stuck. You know, even in my lowest moments I think I always knew I would make it. I'm not the kind of person to ever give up. Life was no fun; I managed to get through my daily routine as a duty more than anything. My family didn't understand and didn't support me at all. They ridiculed the way I ate and thought I was eccentric. I wondered sometimes, too. They were sick of my being sick and were tired of hearing about health things. I longed for my family to say we'll help you or we're here for you, but instead they treated me as if I had a mental problem. Actually, I did have a mental problem; I just didn't realize that the emotional things I had stifled for years were coming through as physical symptoms and would not go away until I had peeled away the layers. But let's put that on hold and get the health store open.

Life is a journey
new paths to be trodden,
with challenges and obstacles
bring opportunities and growing.
Listen to your heart; let your spirit guide you,
and willingly embrace these gifts.
Thank you dear God, for your love...

—CAROLYN PORTER

❧

CHAPTER 6

Transition

It took one year of planning and searching for a location to finally be ready to open our store in the summer of '95. I had better days sometimes but still had many bad days. I kept Xanax around in case I got a "spell" of anxiety (I had worked with an alternative doctor and come off of it again for the last time), but tried not to use it. It was a big change to go to work six days a week and took quite an adjustment given my condition. What I really needed was rest for my adrenals to repair, but that was not to be. There was definitely excitement and a challenge in opening this store. My son and I had a good system: I worked from 10 to 3:15 at which time I left to pick up my daughter from school, and he worked 3 to 8 when the store closed. I didn't know it at the time, but a whole new world was opening up to me. This venture would not only do well but would herald in a total metamorphosis in me.

Opening this store took courage and guts when neither person knew anything about running a business like this. We both had the desire to help people improve and/or maintain their health and we wanted to show how to be physically fit at the same time. Both of us exercised regularly and ate quite healthily, so we had the look of health. I wore make-up, colored my hair and dressed youthfully

⁂

while he shaved, kept his hair short and dressed athletically. We wanted to give this image along with a heart-felt concern for people and their health, and it worked. Our business grew faster than we expected and the whole time we were learning, learning and learning. All this time I was sick. I can remember so many days praying, while driving shakily to work with tears in my eyes, that God would just get me through that day. I will always remember the times when I felt so weak and dizzy that I would lie down on the floor in the backroom of the store and hope no one would come in. Surely someone can help me get well. But the more I researched and learned, the more convinced I became that it was going to be almost entirely up to me to figure my health problems out. I had constant reoccurring symptoms that plagued me, but as time went on I began to have more better days. Once I quit the homeopathic route I definitely improved, but I had gained a wealth of information along the way.

Little did I know what an awesome gift all of this was. Look at all the things I was learning and could in turn help many other people with this knowledge. If I hadn't been sick I probably wouldn't have researched to the depths that I did. Illness of any kind is a wake-up call, a time to re-evaluate what is really important in life. As a result you can wallow in your illness with self-pity and depression or you can take charge and get yourself well. I managed to facilitate both, back and forth, back and forth. It was the beginning of a major shift that would eventually throw me into an entirely different life and perception of life, and the beauty of it all, in hindsight, was that every single step was part of a divine plan. I was strong but I needed to become stronger. I had knowledge but I had to become wiser. I was religious but now I was to become spiritual, and I was anxious but it was essential that I become calm. I was in control but I had to surrender. There was a plan for me that I wasn't aware of and it was unfolding right in front of my eyes. Of course, I was still in the way so I didn't always see the steps, but gradually my eyes began to open.

There was so much to do in the store every day, with ordering and pricing and stocking, and I began to write the newsletters, so that kept me busy reading and studying many books and articles in order to glean the correct information. I was constantly busy and that kept me in a state of being useful and productive. As my son and I gained more knowledge we were able to help more people with their health concerns. We implemented new programs in the store and began preparing to open a second store. I met so many wonderful people and made some dear friends in the process.

However, there was always underlying friction. My husband was a background partner, the bookkeeper, and there were constant problems between the three of us. Perhaps it was the personalities, perhaps it was the very unhappy marriage, perhaps it was the stress involved or perhaps it was just all in the plan. The discord was up and down, but always there.

Another wedding! No.1 son decided it was his time to settle down, but with this wedding I only had to show up! Five children involved in a wedding can be both a blessing and a non-blessing. The blessing was that they filled up half of the bridesmaids and groomsmen but a non-blessing is the cost! It was a gala event and really great as family members once again came together to celebrate. Although my family at home was decreasing in numbers, my extended family was increasing. In a few short months my next daughter would leave home for college. What was I going to do? I guess we'd just keep opening up stores - after all, I loved helping people. However, there was a restlessness stirring in my bones, something that was telling me it was time to move on.

And the day came when the risk to remain tight in a bud was more painful than the risk it took to blossom.

—AUTHOR UNKNOWN

CHAPTER 7

❧

Awakening

Probably the earliest single event that began a subtle awakening in my thought patterns was the day I first went to an intuitive. An intuitive is able to read the positive energy around you and give insights into your life. A customer from my store kept telling me about this man who gave readings and how great he was and that I should go to him and have a reading. I refused; that would have been against my religious beliefs at that time. I told my dearest friend about him and she wanted to go to see him. She kept after me until finally I agreed, mostly out of curiosity and our friendship. The day that I was to see him I was very uneasy, even to the point of being nervous about it, wondering how weird it would be. The intuitive only knew my first name and my birthdate and began talking immediately. The first words out of his mouth were "Congratulations! you have done more in the last two years than most people do in a lifetime, and you deserve the acknowledgement." WOW! What did this man just say to me? He actually applauded me for all I had been through and had done and he didn't even know me. How could this be? What a shock! He talked continuously for a good hour and it was all on tape so I could replay it whenever I wished. That was the beginning of a major shift in how I felt about myself. You see, I realized later that I really didn't

◦⦵◦

think too highly of myself, and this reading made me think maybe I was okay and had done something worthwhile. Oh, don't get me wrong, I had accomplished many things already, but I didn't feel it inside. I had been programmed into believing that I was like a filthy rag deserving the wrath of God, so how could I think I was worth anything? Besides, I was often "rebellious" and therefore punished for that supposed sinfulness of not obeying all the rules. Could it be there were too many rules, too much rigidity, not enough warm, permeating love, or even an incorrect perception? But this man, not knowing anything about me, had made me feel worthy of life and praise for my accomplishments up to then, and even went on to tell me I'd be a speaker to hundreds and even thousands of people. He said I'd write at least one book. The book I could see, maybe, but as for public speaking, I laughed and said no way could I ever be a speaker because I'd be too nervous. What's really funny is that he told me this again when I saw him months later and I laughed again and said, "NEVER"! What's even funnier is the fact that this is exactly what I do now - public speaking!!

Soon after this, through a course of coincidences (oh, I forgot, there are no coincidences!), I began going to a different chiropractor who used alternative health procedures. Under his care I received the greatest health improvement that I had experienced since the beginning of my disorders. However, I certainly can't give him all the credit because in his office was a counselor who I began to see. I knew I needed to end the marriage but was wrestling with guilt, anger, resentment and religious beliefs. Could I justify it? Could I make it on my own? How would the kids adjust? Was I being selfish? Would I be punished?

Of course the counselor would never tell me what I should do, but she made me realize I had layers of deep-seated negative emotions that had to be released. She suggested several books for me to read, and as I did I realized the importance of getting rid of this anger, that it was at the root of many of my physical ailments. I had improved my physical condition with a strict diet but was not well yet. Healing is always a process of balancing mind, body and spirit, so now it was time to address the mind. You'll never guess what I had to do - the impossible! I had to forgive my husband of all those hurts and injustices inflicted on me. How could I ever do that? I had to "let go and let God." As issues surfaced they were released, and forgiveness took their place and my health soared! Many psychologists say that anger is found to be the root cause of depression. As I forgave, it became clear to me that this was a cleansing experience that was needed for complete health. The steps began unfolding until one day I knew, without a shadow of a doubt, that a divorce was necessary. The paragraph that follows I found months later after the divorce proceedings had already begun and all I could say was "Thank you God for waking me up to the potential death of my spirit."

Many basically rational and practical people find that they are unable to leave a relationship even though they can see that it is bad for them...Friends...may have pointed out to them that in reality their "prison door" is wide open and that all they need do is step outside. And yet as desperately unhappy as they are, they hold back. Some of them approach the threshold, then hesitate. Some may make brief sallies outside, but quickly retreat to the safety of prison in relief and despair...Something in them knows that they were not meant to live this way. Yet people in droves choose to remain in their prisons, making no effort to change them—except, perhaps to hang pretty curtains over the bars and paint the walls in decorator colors. They may end up dying in a corner of their cell without having really been alive for years.

—AUTHOR UNKNOWN

The single most life-changing event in my life occurred in September, 1998. I went to a seminar entitled *Breaking The Money Barriers*, presented by Dr. Michael J. Duckett, the founder of this seminar and one of my customers. I heard about money, how to make it, manage it, keep it, invest it, but what stuck in my mind was the perception of life that this man had compared with mine. He presented it with a spiritual foundation and the principles came from God, but were shared in a way that was totally different from anything I had ever heard. Dr. Duckett had endured so much more in just his childhood than I had in my entire life up to then, yet he was loving and giving and happy. As the weeks went by I couldn't get that seminar out of my mind. I knew then I wanted whatever it was that he had. I wanted to feel all that genuine love so I could give it out as he did. I wanted to be happy from the inside. He had taught in the seminar that everything is done from the inside out, even to bringing the money into your life, and that you do it one little step at a time.

So I took that first step and it felt okay, not bad in fact. I started making changes in my attitude and I started smiling more. I tried to think of my problems as an opportunity to learn and grow instead of this heavy weight on my shoulders. I felt better. I began to notice positive changes in the way I responded to things and people and I noticed that the people responded back more positively. If you're smiling at someone it often makes them return one to you. That one smile can become contagious and affect 10,000 people! As you change, you encourage change in everyone around you, especially your family. It was a good change but they weren't sure how to react at first. Of course I slipped back into my old nature frequently at the beginning, but gradually I improved. But I had a lot to face and it was fast approaching. Change was in the air and I would never be the same again!

⁂

I began talking to my children, one at a time, indicating to them what I was about to do, and to my utter amazement I received comments such as: "What took you so long (32 years)," "It's about time," and "We wondered if you'd ever have enough guts to do it!" Nothing is hidden from your children. They were as miserable as I was. You could cut the tension in the house with a knife - lots of negative energy. Many things poured out from my children as they revealed their inner thoughts, and I remember saying I had chosen years earlier to stay for them, to which one said "You shouldn't have." I had done what I thought was for the good of all, but looking back at that point I wondered if I wasn't more afraid than anything. Probably it was a mixture of reasons but what I was forgetting was, this was exactly the right time for this to take place. I had no reason to feel guilty for waiting so long or guilty for the misery my children had endured. I had tried and learned and grown, however slowly, and now it was time to say, "This is enough." I can say with a 100 percent honesty that never once did I ever regret making this decision. It felt right and it was right, and everyone involved saw the benefits of this decision. No one wants to see a marriage break up, but was it really a marriage? No, not at all, all that really broke up was the contract, the piece of paper. The real connection that is important for a marriage to work was never there in the first place, so there was nothing to break up.

Two lives with energy unite
whose souls could not connect,
never sharing, never healing, never growing,
prisoners of their own dying love.
To remain would have been the
sad, slow dance of death.

—CAROLYN PORTER

CHAPTER 8

Disconnection

A divorce is always hard no matter how bad the marriage. There is still the reality of something together, in whatever form, being torn asunder. If you ever divorce, do not involve your kids in it. At the beginning I shared the goings-on with my children and that was a mistake; so did their dad. You see, they are in the middle and you don't want to put them in the situation where they have to take sides. It isn't fair to them. Most of my children were adults at the time so it was different than with younger children. I wanted people to talk to but they were the wrong ones, even though they validated many things for me. It puts a lot of tension into their lives that they shouldn't have to deal with. After all, they already have the divorce itself to handle. So talk to friends, clergy, counselors, whomever, but not your kids.

The divorce itself was uneventful. I made up my mind that I would be as congenial as was possible and also fair. As I left the judge's chamber after the final decree was issued, my attorney asked me how I felt. I thought a minute and replied - sad but at the same time happy. It was over and now on to a new life. As I drove back to work a wave of emptiness came over me, as if I wasn't connected to anything anymore. But the marriage was only held together by a thread before, so why this feeling? This is a natural feeling that happens to many people in a divorce. You are used to this particular way of life, no matter how miserable, and now it's all changed. Change is good, but you have to fix your mindset to accept it as good. I knew that inside, but now I had to deal with that feeling of actually being alone. At least before there had been someone in the house. I had really never had to take care of myself. It meant I had to buy a house myself, take care of insurances, fix things (I got to know the guys in Home Depot well) hang shelves, use a drill, put molly bolts into the wall and hang drapes, paint, cut the grass, and so on. It was exciting but I felt overwhelmed - so much new, so much to learn. I had to be strong for myself and for my children.

Four of them helped me move - it took four loads in the U-haul and two 15-hour days to accomplish. It was a big change from the big house we had to the small one I had purchased, but it was mine. I thought I would miss that beautiful house I had spent so many hours decorating but, except for my eyes filling up as I drove away for the last time, I can honestly say I never thought of that house again. A house is just a thing, the home is in the heart. Three of my children were living with me at the time of the move, although one would leave soon for college. I wondered how they would adjust to being in a small house and farther away from friends, but the second night, as we sat at our dinner table eating, one of them said, "Mom, this is really nice, I like it here, it's peaceful." My heart was about to burst and I was so proud of my kids. They had come through it all so well and I told them so. At that moment I realized anew how richly blessed I was with these wonderful blessings.

Now adjustment time. No matter how much you want a divorce, how good it is for both of you or how ready you are for it, there are always adjustments. I felt fear at all the extra respon-

❧

sibilities because of my lack of knowledge in areas that I now had control over. For the first few weeks I would burst into tears for no reason other than being alone and frightened. This would happen at least once per day. One child saw me at the kitchen sink as she went up the stairs (I was looking out the window hoping she didn't notice) and said, "Are you crying mom?" I answered, "Not really"(a really brilliant comment). She replied, "What's wrong with you, you cry every day?" My lame answer was just, "Something at work; I'll be fine." How do you explain to a young person the overwhelming feeling of responsibility or the feeling of not belonging anywhere anymore? Who was I and where did I fit? What would my life be like? Would I meet someone else down the road and have a great relationship? After all, my children would be gone in a couple of years and it would really get lonely to be by myself. What about finances, would I make it when the child support and alimony stopped in a couple years? So many questions that didn't have an answer. Where was my faith? Why couldn't I trust that? And where was Carolyn? What did I want my life to be? What I didn't know was that a whole new world was about to open up that would trigger a complete metamorphosis of my soul and my heart. I would finally know who I am and my purpose on this planet.

♥ YOUR HEART KNOWS ♥

Trust your heart; it speaks to you.

Know life holds wonderful mysteries.

Live each day in joyous wonderment.

Unlease your soul and fly free.

Each day is a new beginning; know that today is all that you have.

You hold the paintbrush, create your dreams.

Know the enchantment of life.

Obstacles are opportunities to grow.

Perfection is not of this world. Accept you just as you are.

Angel wings encircle you.

Rainbows come after the storm.

Your spirit knows how special you are.

One smile lights up 10,000 faces.

Coincidences are God's miracles.

Miracles happen to those who believe.

Always know there are miracles!

—CAROLYN PORTER

CHAPTER 9

Miracles

On July 3, 1999, something happened that would change my life forever. Never would I be the same again, my life would change dramatically. This would bring continuous miracles. I received a letter from Dr. Michael J. Duckett, the founder of the same seminar that I attended that had started the changes in me, and he was inviting me to train under him, along with 21 other hand-picked people, to be certified to teach the *Breaking The Money Barriers* Seminar that had helped me so much. As I read the letter an incredible wave of fear went all through me and I put it down. What was he thinking? I could never do that. The seminar is four hours long! Did he really think I could ever stand up in front of people and talk for four hours? I'd be a nervous wreck, I'd probably faint. I went about putting away my groceries and eating dinner while listening to some classical music, intent on relaxing in a bit with a book I had out to start reading. But I couldn't get that letter out of my mind, still thinking I could never do it. Finally I went and picked up the letter and read it again and I saw something that I hadn't caught before - he said pray about it. I hadn't thought of that. So, being a praying person, I decided I'd try that avenue, knowing of course that the answer was already no. However, as I prayed, I felt this tugging in my heart and a feeling I should do this. After all, look at all the changes that had occurred in my life after attending his seminar; I could help others do the same. But then I thought again of the fear and how I could never get up in front of people and speak. So now it's no again. Then I recalled how Dr. Duckett had addressed fear and mentioned that when you take action the fear goes away because it's only a product of your imagination. Then I thought, this is not imagination - I'm scared just thinking about it! The book was never opened and after a while Beethoven's Fifth Symphony became too much for my pounding head. Something inside kept saying I should do this but I knew I couldn't. It was back and forth and back and forth, a mental battle that raged on and on and I couldn't seem to stop. So I decided to paint my kid's bathroom. No one would be home for two days and I had to do something so why not. I hate to paint but I knew I couldn't sleep. Besides, if I wanted it painted I now had to do it myself. This would be easier since I was sponge painting after the base coat. I decided to do the base coat and then go to bed, but the raging war continued so I painted all the coats of sponging also. Finally, at 3 a.m. I decided to try to sleep with the aid of some herbs. They kept me asleep for barely two hours and the first thought that popped into my mind was no, I can't do this. Besides, he is a brilliant, world-renowned speaker, how could I ever present a seminar that would come close to his? No, there is no way; it's definitely no. About 8 a.m. with tears still wetting my face, an unbelievable feeling came over me and I was "told" to go ahead and do this training and all I had to do was take the step and I would be helped. I had been praying for new doors to open but this was not what I had in mind. I felt relief, fear and fatigue all at the same moment. Over the next few days I seesawed back and forth, but I knew deep down inside if I really listened, that the answer had to be yes. Finally, I called and said okay, I'll do it.

❧

It would involve an entire weekend for the training; I wasn't sure all that would be involved, but I knew I had to speak in front of everyone and I was getting nervous already. When the day came for the training I was petrified and didn't think I'd be able to stand up front and do it; my legs were literally shaking, so when you use the phrase shaking in your boots, I can vouch for knowing this reality. There were eight speeches for each person over the two days, only a few minutes each, and as we started the second round of speaking he asked for volunteers. To my utter amazement I jumped up and said I wanted to get this over with so I'd go first. This was not me who jumped up; somebody else made this happen. Everyone there must have known how nervous I was - it was a little obvious I think - so when I jumped up they all applauded. I was stunned. Why did they all do that? I felt embarrassed and at the same time elated. Anyway, I made it through the weekend and it got easier, no more shaking legs. This was nothing short of a miracle!

I set my first seminar for eight weeks away. I had to rewrite the entire seminar into my own words, using my own stories and my terminology to some degree. I found it difficult at first, but the more I prayed the more it flowed. I received much encouragement from Dr. Duckett and friends. I kept visualizing myself presenting it with ease and having no difficulty speaking. We'll see if this works!

I rehearsed constantly. I walk two to three miles about five times each week, so as I walked I rehearsed. I remained pretty calm until three hours before time to start and then it hit me. I got a headache and started shaking; my legs felt rubbery and tears welled up. My hands were cold and sweaty. The next thing I knew it was time to walk up to the podium. My heart was pounding and my mouth dry; I just knew I'd never be able to stand up there for four hours. For about twenty minutes I was

❧

aware of these symptoms, finally taking a drink of water to ease the dry mouth. I looked at the clock and was in total shock - two hours had gone by! What had happened here? The fear had gone. I went into action teaching a life-changing message and the fear had vanished. Could this really be? I finished with such ease and, other than a few moments of apprehension before each seminar, it gives me no problem. The visualization helped tremendously and I know speaking and teaching are definitely my calling. Isn't it amazing what can happen when you let go? What if I had never taken that first step? What a different turn my life would have taken. Yes, I do believe in miracles!

A few weeks went by after my seminar and I noticed changes beginning in some of the attendees. Wow! The message I had shared had been absorbed and lives were changing. I began to see a sparkle in their eyes and all I could say was "Thank you, God." A couple of the people had learned what their life purpose should be and were pursuing it. They were radiating happiness. The inner joy I felt was beyond words - realizing I had helped these folks get on the right track. It was incredible. I knew without a shadow of a doubt that I had made the right choice. Never in a million years would I have ever chosen this avenue of service. By letting go my entire life changed from the inside out. Now I could help many people and I loved it.

I was planning seminars, working in the store six days a week and taking care of my family. A restless feeling was knawing at me inside, telling me it was time to move on and take a step out in faith. "Restlessness is God tugging at our hearts and telling us to step out in faith" is a saying I heard at that time that stayed with me. So, after utilizing the inner-battle strategy once again, I made the decision to leave the stores, and although I remained an owner, my sons now handled the stores.

Let's review the last nine months of my life. My dad, who

always listened and helped with his advice, had died. I was now divorced, had moved my residence and now was not just changing my job but changing my entire career. These are four of the top 10 most traumatic experiences that can occur in a person's life, and they had all happened to me in less than a year. No wonder my adrenals had a hard time healing. I was totally out of my comfort zone and becoming very spiritual, not just religious. Nothing in my life was the same - just a bit unnerving. However, as I began to shift my mindset I realized what a blessing all of this was and a major opportunity for growth. I was being given a chance for a completely different life from what I had ever previously experienced, a gift from God. It was like starting over again, as if I had just graduated from college and was heading out into the world. As I thought of it that way I became very excited and that excitement poured out of me. I was interested in community things and began to use my piano-playing ability, although a bit rusty, in retirement homes where it is so appreciated. I felt so much love for these seniors and I began to feel love and concern for everyone I knew and met. I noticed how life was exciting and challenging. Miracle upon miracle was happening. It was beyond anything I had ever experienced. I have a purpose, to love, serve and give to others and this is required of all of us. What had happened to that thought pattern of mine when I asked what I would do with my life after my kids were gone and the marriage was over? I had been so worried about what I would or wouldn't have that I forgot the real purpose in life - to give of yourself in love. What a difference it makes when you change your thoughts. Life has a whole new meaning. What if I had said no to the question asked in that letter back on July 3, 1999?

This is a skeletal overview of my life up to now, but never again will I say no because of fear or feeling inadequate. Here I am, writing this book - another dream. I had planned to write a book on

⚭

health but the message came to me to write this one now. I have many more goals and as God directs I will pursue them.

This concludes the first part of my story, but now we'll look at the lessons to be learned from these eventful years. The words that fell onto these pages came through me to you. My prayer is that you will open your heart to allow them to penetrate deep into your soul.

PART II

Awareness

PREFACE

❧

Each of us makes a difference in this world and each of us has a purpose for our life. Many people go through life never realizing either of these. How sad. I thought my purpose, although I never thought of it as a purpose before, was to be a wife and mother and piano teacher. At that time in my life it was, but God had placed many gifts inside me as He does in us all. I hadn't fully realized these talents in myself until one by one circumstances occurred which awakened me to see new potentials. So many times people fail to see the signs, but more often than not they see them but are not motivated to implement them. They are comfortable floating through life, taking but not giving. What can I get out of this life, not what can I give to this life. What's in it for me? How much money can I make? How many friends can I have? How much fun can I have? How successful can I become? If you don't jump out of bed every morning excited to see what doors God will open for you today in which you can serve others, then I challenge your inner happiness and fulfillment.

Awareness is the first step for making changes in our lives. If we aren't aware, how could we learn how to prevent problems in our lives? After recognizing there is an obstacle, we must accept it. Acceptance involves the realization that it is ours and ours alone; no one else can change our lives or do the repair work.

Life is meant to be a celebration, not a drudgery. Judging from the number of long faces and the vast amount of antidepressants prescribed daily by physicians, not too many people are celebrating life. Too many problems, you say, or too many stresses. That's the typical mindset. But wait, our thoughts control our words and actions which in turn create our life. So maybe we need to change our thought patterns. Try this the next time you face a problem or obstacle - treat it as an opportunity to learn and grow. Dissect it and pull out every lesson you can and then you've changed a negative into a positive. It deflates that heavy burden on your shoulder and life takes on a new dimension. Isn't that really what problems are, a chance to grow? Some people seem to have more problems than others. Maybe they have more lessons to learn or maybe God has big plans for them. The more chances they have for growth the stronger and more productive they can become. These obstacles are actually gifts from God because through the obstacles we can shine if we learn the lesson. As I continue with part II of this book I will show you many obstacles in my life that most likely are evident in your own life as well. These once stood in my way, blocking me from being the whole, happy, fulfilled person I now am. I'll also guide you into ways of unblocking your negative emotions so that your soul can fly free and your heart can open, pouring out unconditional love to the world. It is then that happiness and fulfillment become your greatest reward. That, my dear friends, is how life becomes a celebration!

*Opening your mind
opening your heart
brings blessings from God
and new possibilities.*

—CAROLYN PORTER

CHAPTER 10

❧

Holding On

A ccording to Webster's dictionary, controlling means having authority, directing, managing, having power, governing, commanding; you get the picture. This I choose to address first because everyone does this in varying degrees, and relinquishing control is extremely difficult for most people to do. Everyone instinctively wants power, to be the boss, to be respected. Obviously, some folks utilize this characteristic in a recognizable way, but often it is used in subtle ways that sneak into life situations without being observed. Control can be used in a very manipulative way to get what we want or to get a desired result. It can often be used without conscious awareness of what is happening.

One way control is evident is through shame. Shame is a core emotion from which many other negative emotions receive their energy. Shame is feeling disgraced, humiliated, defective, blameworthy, accompanied with wanting to cover up or hide. Shame causes someone to live defensively, and an individual who feels shamed will have a desire to control to cover that shame. It is a very destructive force and, because it is a secret emotion, it is most crippling to the human spirit.

Most shame is called a "family inheritance" because it is often

❄

cultivated in our early life experiences. Things that are called inherited shames involve bankruptcies, suicides, childhood deaths or accidents in which the parents feel at fault, or secrets around pregnancies, births and adoptions. Other secrets that create a feeling of shame surround alcoholism, addictions of all types, abuse, adultery, past prison terms, instances of abandonment, or even illnesses, binding them by that power. A woman who feels this shame often becomes a rescuer and marries a man who needs help.

Another source of shame is unresolved grief. This source is evident when someone feels responsible for another person's misfortune or even death, an example of which might be a survivor in an accident feeling guilty that he/she is alive. Another example could be a sibling who always excels, making the other sibling feel shamed since they see the pride their parents show to that sibling, making them feel unworthy. If a child is shamed the message comes through loud and clear that he is flawed or defective and this creates guilt in him. This guilt sabatoges his healthy emotional growth, creating deeply embedded scars of low self-esteem that may last a lifetime.

Perhaps a parent has high expectations of you but you have trouble meeting those expectations, whether they be in sports, academics, life vocation or whatever. So you feel guilty and then shameful because you can't or don't choose to live up to their goals. In my own life I never felt I measured up. My parents had high religious standards and I never could please them although I tried. Remember all my incidences! They wanted me to go into full-time Christian service, even to being a missionary, but I had no desire for that. Because I chose other areas for my vocation and seemed to frequently break the "rules," I was full of shame and guilt. Remember also, I was nothing more than a filthy rag according to the religious teachings of my parents, so how could

❧

I ever amount to anything? The only way to become better was to confess my sin and be saved, which I did, but that didn't remedy those secret emotions. They went with me into adulthood and stayed within me until I realized I wasn't required to do things their way. I am a unique, magnificently created human being who has to decide what life has to be. So what did I do? I tried to control my life and my own family in order to feel worthy. I did, however, recognize some of that controlling aspect so that I never implemented it to the same extent as I had experienced. Fortunately, as the years went by, I let go of trying to control my children and let them become who they want to become. When one dropped out of college I stated only once that I wished it didn't happen, but allowed that child to make his/her own decision. We can guide and that's all we can do. Sometimes when one of my children quit a job or wanted to trade in a car too soon, I advised them a certain way but usually allowed them to make the decision. How else will they ever learn unless they get to choose their own experiences and lessons? They aren't always wise choices, so they learn from them and then they grow.

Let's examine how shame manifests as control in our lives. One of the ways is perfectionism. If a person feels flawed or imperfect they will try to hide it and attempt to be perfect or do things perfectly so as not to be exposed. They live in a state of fear that they can't be perfect. Of course they can't be perfect so that brings up the issue of low self-worth. This is one of the biggest problems in our society today - low self-esteem. We are taught that when we perform well, or perfectly, we win approval and love. That is love with conditions. The parents, for example, may really love their child but portray that accomplishing certain goals allows more love to flow from them. That's why a sibling who always lives in the shadow of a gifted and often praised sibling can feel so grieved and shamed. Remember when I actually

⚭

hammered my finger to break it so that I wouldn't have to enter that piano contest? I was afraid of failing, or not doing a bang-up job (did you catch that?). Where do you think that thought pattern came from? Was I born with it? Possibly, but more than likely it was programmed into me as a child to keep striving for perfection in keeping God's commands, but knowing all the time I could never attain that. Don't forget I never could measure up to their religious goals. Didn't God create us in His own image? Would He create something that wasn't valuable? Do you think He loves some of us more than others? God loves us all equally and we are all valuable. Some have more gifts than others but we are all responsible for making use of our God-given talents. Does He expect perfection? Of course not, but we are required to keep working on it and improve ourselves daily. We are not to walk in someone else's footsteps but to walk in our own and learn as we go. Perfection will never be attained on this earth but only in heaven.

Another way shame is manifested is through addictions. People who feel great shame have a hard time dealing with life and often resort to drugs, alcohol, work, food, even excessive shopping or sexual behaviors. This is how they cover up that deeply embedded shame so that they can escape from the pain. As I explain to you in part III, it is very painful to bring this shame up to the surface and release it, but it's the only way to heal your life.

I have always loved being busy and I imagine I always will. I love to be productive and create things and watch things come together. This is evident in my whole life, but it was often overdone. I needed praise to feel better about myself so I would drive myself to accomplish more and more. I always wanted to achieve as much as I could, but some of it was excessive and it was never enough. I could never measure up because all that shame and guilt was still buried and it was controlling my life. It was one of the factors that made my health deteriorate, a pointed, yet constructive wake up call.

Rage is considered one of the most naturally occurring cover-ups for shame and it often appears in the form of blame or criticism. Have you ever heard a parent say: "Why can't you get good grades like your sister?" That criticism is a rage coming from inside because of his own shame and unworthiness. Negative patterns from parents are programmed into the next generation, which just continues the cycle. These shame-based patterns make you a controlling woman who always needs to be in charge of a situation, otherwise you show your vulnerability. This means controlling thoughts, feelings and actions, not just of yourself but also of others. It's not a controlling driven by power but rather wishing for respect and safety. Often we discipline our children in a way so they know who's boss, especially if we are irritated or angry when we do the disciplining. Where's the love? It's the love that makes someone want to do what you wish them to do, not fear. Granted, you may get the desired response with fear but it won't be because they want to obey you but, rather, fear the consequences. It's all in how you present the discipline.

It's a difficult journey releasing this buried shame and sometimes it takes a long time to realize your worth. We will take a look at this process in the chapter, Peeling Away the Layers.

With force it erupts
or silent and brewing
it slowly destroys our soul.
— CAROLYN PORTER

CHAPTER 11

&

Eaten Alive

Another form of using the control trap is with anger. Anger is the strongest emotion says Barbara Sullivan in *The Control Trap*, and makes the strongest impression. It is the quickest way to make a point and say "Pay attention to me!"

There are three major ways a woman's anger can control a man. Men by nature don't want to fight with a woman, mainly because of their physical strength. Of course a woman usually outdoes the man in a verbal fight! To combat this, some men resort to physical abuse but more often than not express passive/aggressive behavior by tuning you out and becoming quiet.

Secondly, a man doesn't want to make a woman cry; it goes against his protective drive. Crying when angry or fighting is a common female tactic. I had a friend who always used tears to get male sympathy and get her way. It worked twice when she was stopped by a policeman for speeding. She let those tears flow and the officer felt sorry for her and gave her a warning. Of course I never did anything like that!

Sometimes a man is afraid a woman may leave him if she gets angry enough, so she is rewarded for emotional outbursts. Maybe he gets her flowers to appease her or just gives in so that she gets her way. That is pure manipulation, a very common

❧

practice in a relationship but very destructive.

There are three branches of anger. The first is the emotional branch. Anger is viewed as a masculine emotion and for a woman to display anger it is considered by most as unfeminine. This anger is often converted into more acceptable feelings such as guilt or hurt. So what happens to all that anger? It is buried, or stuffed away. This suppressed anger eats away at your soul and often turns into depression. A psychologist and educator, Paul J. Gelinas, says, "In many years as a clinical psychologist working with young adults, I cannot recall a single case of neurosis or emotional disturbance that did not have unresolved anger as the main overt or intrinsic element in the disorder."

When anger is turned inwards it affects the emotional communication we give off to others by our looks, words and body language. You know those looks that could kill, the daggers in the eyes, or maybe it's the little "digs" you keep throwing out. Perhaps you slam things around or give the silent treatment or go and pout. All of these are manifestations of buried anger, a little more sneaky than explosive anger. All of this creates continuous negative energy around us. Whatever dominates your conscious thoughts will control your emotions and therefore your actions.

Once anger manifests in the physical realm the affects can be staggering. Anger is the most powerful emotion. The New England Journal of Medicine states that suppressed hostility is the main cause of insomnia, fatigue, headaches, ulcers, high blood pressure, heart attacks and cancer. Our bodies are made of interacting fields of energy, and anger or other negative emotions will block the flow of energy, stimulating or influencing the disease process.

In a book called *Heartmath Solutions*, the author gives us some alarming statistics concerning anger and its effects on the heart and our health. Our body's stress response encompasses more

⚬

than 1,400 known physical and chemical reactions and over 30 different hormones and neurotransmitters. Adrenaline, noradrenaline and cortisol are activated under stress even hours after the stress has occurred. It sears the body like acid. Negative emotions, such as anger and fear, cause an increase in irregular heart rhythms which affect the entire body and the nervous system. Emotional stress waves are like earthquake waves - they vibrate for days! Did you realize that talking about something that made you angry can actually reinforce your original feeling and do your body more harm than your first response? This is scary! Just think of how many angry people you know. The sad thing is they are on the road to their own destruction.

Anger also affects our spiritual life. We certainly can't be close to God if we're angry. This anger reveals itself in two forms, frustration and inferiority. When our needs are not met we often become frustrated. When you can't figure out a math problem and throw the book across the room, that's frustration. In the early months of my marriage, when I was extremely agitated with my husband one time, I kicked the bedroom door and to my horror my foot went through it. It wasn't that I was super strong or anything; it was simply one of those cheap apartment doors. What did this incident gain me? Nothing positive, that's for sure. Not only did I feel bad for my outburst, there was an added expense with the repair. This is a good example of strong frustration! Some folks allow frustration to fester for years, maybe after being overlooked for a promotion or a so-called friend who procrastinates about paying back a loan to you.

Then there's inferiority. When we don't feel respected by others and are constantly criticized, our worth is lessened and we feel inferior. As I mentioned previously, low self-esteem is one of the biggest problems in our society today. We have been negatively programmed, unintentionally of course, mostly by our parents.

⌘

When we don't feel good about ourselves we naturally don't handle stress as well. It keeps us in a constant negative state as far as self-confidence and achievement go. Many times it keeps us from even trying things because we feel we're not good enough. This can be a real problem in a relationship because we tend to want the other person to make us feel good, making them responsible. Inferiority, like these other negative emotions, literally affects every aspect of our lives.

Most anger is rooted in the past and usually requires the releasing of many stored emotions. This release will be discussed in Part III of this book.

Grasping and holding back, fear chokes our dreams,
blocking our potential;
shackled like prisoners, as life slowly fades,
wasting our gifts, the world will never see.
It's only a thought we imagine!

—CAROLYN PORTER

CHAPTER 12

Our Biggest Barrier

False evidence about reality, that's fear. Fear is nothing more than a product of our imagination, an illusion, something not even real. We think we're afraid of something, judging the outcome, and it's not even reality and probably will never happen. But yet this thing called fear holds us back from so many things as it hinders our development and ability to be of use to others. Although it's imaginary it affects real life.

Do you realize we're born with only one fear, and that's the fear of loud noises? So where do the rest of our fears come from? They are taught to us and programmed into us - all of them. Then we in turn pass them on to our offspring and the cycle continues.

People fear everything from not enough money to the safety of their children, old age, their health, dogs, storms, driving in traffic, going to the dentist, public speaking, keeping their job and the bogey man! What do we gain from all this fear? Nothing positive for sure. It keeps us in a negative mode, all closed up.

When we allow fear to grasp our life we are limiting our growth and what we can be. Think of it as a vice that keeps you firmly confined to the same space, not going anywhere. Every time we say I can't, we allow fear to be in control; we're allowing self-sabatoge. A quote I use in one of the seminars I give is, "He

☙

who is afraid of a thing gives it power over him." Is that what you want to do with your life, give the control to fear?

We talked about self-worth and inferiority in the last chapter, and when we allow fear to diminish our potential, we are feeding our low self-worth. Just think of how many things you have passed up due to the fact you didn't think you could accomplish them. You have limited yourself all because of a mistaken perception of the meaning of truth.

As a child I feared my dad. He was stern, rigid, very serious and he ruled with an iron hand. There were many rules and as you recall I seemed to break quite a few along the way. All my mom would have to say was, "Wait 'til your dad gets home; he'll take care of this," and I'd get those rubbery legs. Sure enough, when he got home, he took care of it! First there would be a discussion, better described as a sermon about how I had sinned and how God required punishment for sin, and because he loved me he had to punish me. Then he'd discuss the punishment I deserved for the error of my ways. He believed in spare the rod and you spoil the child, so I often preferred a cushion to a wooden seat for an hour or two. Sometimes he reacted quicker and the discussion came afterwards. This was love? My dad thought so, but in my heart it didn't feel like love at all. Maybe it's just a different way to express love from a different perception. All my life I've tried to reason with this interpretation, but have come to the conclusion that lovingly discussing the incident, incorporating the child's perspective as well as the parent's, reaps far better results without damaging the self-worth of the child. A consequence may be necessary, but in love, not fear.

Rules, rules and more rules. Are they all necessary? I used to think so. I had so many rules with five kids it was hard to keep up with all of the rules and who broke them. By the third child I was reducing them, but it wasn't until later I realized there were

❦

way too many. How could anyone enjoy life with so many rules? You couldn't. Don't get me wrong, there must be rules - I prefer to call them guidelines. I also feel there must be consequences for not conforming to the guidelines, but take the fear out and really show love instead. If you talk to my older children they will tell you how much easier I am on the younger siblings. This happens in most families. The kids think it's not fair, but they will probably do the same thing. We grow as we mature.

Always do what you say. If you tell a child about the consequence that will occur should the guidelines be broken, but don't follow through, you are giving mixed signals and definitely tearing down his respect for your rules and thus his self-worth. Have you ever heard a parent shout out something like, "You'd better do what I say or I'm going to break your neck?" Of course most people aren't really going to break the child's neck, so why say it? It sounds impressive, right? It's that control thing again or the "I'm in charge" attitude. It shows ignorance, impatience and a lack of security in that adult in obtaining the desired results unless he/she feels in control. Using this means of control is an aspect of fear.

Obviously there are circumstances where fear is a valid emotion. For instance, if someone is holding a knife at your throat or you're being chased or you just avoided being involved in a car accident, then fear is justified. When I was 10, a 42 year old man tried to get me into his car with the intention of rape. Thankfully I was able to escape, but I can assure you my heart was about to pop out of my chest with the fear I was feeling. Another similar incident happened when I was sixteen. Remember I traveled two hours each way to and from school during my high school years and I played field hockey. Sometimes we had a late game so that meant I traveled home at 9:30 p.m. or later. I was waiting for the bus with only a few people around one night, when a man came

✂

from nowhere and grabbed me and began molesting me. Talk about justifiable fear! But once again my guardian angels were with me and I escaped. Those high spirits I was born with helped again. Needless to say I fought, big-time!

That brings me to another point. When we go into action the fear either goes away completely or is reduced to being manageable. When I was preparing to give my first seminar, which would mean I'd have to stand in front of people for four hours and talk, I kept thinking I'd never be able to do it. However, I kept visualizing myself presenting the seminar with ease and when I got up to present it for the first time, after about 20 minutes the fear dissipated and I enjoyed it. Just think what I would have missed if I had never tried it! Not only that, the people who attended would not have heard the information that I presented to help them change and improve their lives. So the next time something enters your path that you'd like to do or feel you should do, DO IT! Step out in faith that God and the angels will help you. Yes, I definitely believe in angels; they are my constant companions and help me every hour of every day. Even if you don't believe in them, they are by your side waiting to help you.

Taking action helps to eradicate fear, but there are other measures you can implement also. Create a plan or an alternative to your fear and turn it into a positive. Maybe you are afraid of putting on weight. An alternative would be to educate yourself on exercising modalities and proper nutritional habits to prevent this perceived weight gain problem.

Another way is to dissect this fear and ask why you are so fearful. I used to be extremely fearful of going to the dentist and would get myself in a frenzy when I had to go. After learning about fear by attending Dr. Duckett's seminar on fear, I thought about it and how to get rid of it; I literally pulled it apart. What did I really fear? Was it the pain? No, because you can have a shot if it hurts. Was it the dentist? No, I really like her, so it wasn't that. What was it? I finally figured out that it was more of a psychological problem. It was the confinement, of sitting still while your head is held down. So I talked to my dentist about it, only to find out she felt the same way, so she said if I start feeling confined to hold my finger up and she'll give me a break - that's what she does. I only had to hold my finger up one time despite having a great deal of restorative work done. (I had all the toxic amalgam fillings taken out and replaced with composites that are non-toxic and also had all the crowns changed.) So all that fear was nothing more than a product of my imagination with no real grounds for it!

Another way to either eliminate or reduce your fear is to change your focus. Obviously if you are constantly thinking of what you are afraid of it is dominating your thoughts and you are actually creating the exact scenario in your life that you don't want. This is where the power of your mind comes in. NEVER underestimate the power of your mind because whatever you are thinking is what creates your life. As I mentioned earlier, I was very afraid of public speaking, but I was committed to doing it so therefore became determined to accomplish it. I began the visualization of presenting the seminar with ease, but I also used positive affirmations such as, "I am teaching this seminar to these people who need this information to change their lives and I'm doing it easily and enjoying it." I repeated it out loud many times a day for several weeks. Then of course there was prayer, lots of it. I hadn't started meditating at that time but I would utilize that to help eradicate any fear. God helped, as He always does. A thought to remember is no one can think in your mind but you, and whatever you think, so it is!

An additional means to help your fears disappear is to make use of three lists. In the first list name your fears, in the second

჻

list tell where they came from if you know and, in the third list, write what life would be like without this fear. When you take action like this you actually deflate the fear. Replace that fear with a positive statement of how you would feel without it and then change your thought patterns. This takes discipline and perseverance, but now you are on your way to overcoming it because you're in charge.

All of these negative emotions we have been discussing, shame, anger, blame, low self-esteem, fear, are forms of self-sabatoge. We put ourselves down saying we can't accomplish something when we could probably do just that. I could have used this thought pattern when I was considering whether or not to start teaching seminars and, believe me, I have been guilty of using self-sabatoge many times before. But this time I listened to that inner voice. Do you have any idea of the feeling of freedom I feel knowing that I'm doing what I'm supposed to do?

What peace! Once the first step is taken, doors continually open in additional directions and each step of faith gets easier and easier. Is your life exciting and adventurous or are you stuck in the same hum-drum existence, having been there for years, perhaps? If you are comfortable and there is no resistance or change, you are not growing, because growth always requires change, getting out of your comfort zone. Are you a prisoner of your own mind, limiting yourself and the endless possibilities beyond your wildest dreams?

You do realize procrastination is simply self-sabatoge, so every time you say I'll start next week on that exercise program or I've got to do this before I can begin whatever, or I'm too old or too tired, you are sabatoging yourself. You must first become aware of this self-defeating act and then change your thought processes. Begin using positive affirmations to utilize your new thought concepts. "Affirmations ignite passion, passion fuels action, and

✂

action brings opportunities," is a great quote from Dr. Duckett. I use this over and over. Focus on how it will feel to succeed as you accomplish your goals, like work in the job you love and have always wanted to do or find that perfect partner or lose those extra unwanted pounds. **Believe it, say it, write it, see it and make it your reality.** You hold the paint brush in your hand and the canvas is right in front of you. It's totally up to you what strokes or colors you use and what picture will be the end result. Make it beautiful; dream your dreams; make them come true!

Happiness flows from within your own heart,
leaning on others loses your soul;
an empowered life risks letting go.

—CAROLYN PORTER

CHAPTER 13

Hanging On

Most of us travel through life believing that someone or something will make us happy. We wait and pray and wait some more, but somehow happiness eludes us. If we just had a wonderful partner in our life, or had more money, or could get that promotion, or have more relaxation time, or if our health was better...then, we could be happy. That is an illusion! An illusion is a false perception or an unreal interpretation of what one sees. There is absolutely no one in this world who can make you happy nor anything tangible that can do that either. Happiness comes from deep within you, deep in your soul and your heart; it is the result of living on purpose, doing what you know you should be doing as you love and serve people. This is true happiness and fulfillment in life.

That statement kind of pulls the rug out from under, since many women think it's their partner or children or status or career that makes them happy. These are just the icing on the cake. They add to our happiness, but real happiness is something you have to create for yourself. This feeling that someone else is responsible for your happiness is why so many women are codependent on men. We can turn this equation around because men are very often codependent on women, too!

❧

Women are brought up to believe that their main job in life is to marry, satisfy their husband, take care of him, run the household, manage the kids, be the chauffeur, cook, housekeeper etc., and sometimes work in a job outside the home. All of this keeps her a caretaker and usually codependent on her family and their needs. Many women think this is their purpose in life. It may be your responsibility and desire at one point in your life, but you always have your own spirit that should be nourished and growing. This is where the problem is. It certainly was in my life. A woman can easily lose herself in caring for everyone else and never realize her God-given abilities that she needs to use as she helps others. Each woman and each man has a distinct calling in this life and so many never even think about it, let alone realize it and take the action steps to make it happen.

Codependency is a difficult thing to address; it's one of those fuzzy, gray areas. Most people think of codependency as an addiction problem like alcohol, drugs or nicotine, but it involves so much more than those. Codependency affects many, many people.

So what is codependency? Codependency is a behavior that we learn or a defect in our character that prevents us or reduces our capacity to be a participant in loving relationships. It's saying, I'm a caretaker, I'm married to an alcoholic or troubled person, feeling that all your relationships end up the same way so that you feel trapped, or needing someone to grab on to.

I really believe codependency is basically allowing someone else's behavior to affect you and control your life because you are obsessed with controlling that person's life. Wow! That statement applies to the majority of people who inhabit this planet at one time or another!

How did so many people become codependent? It is a learned pattern or behavior; we learn it from our parents mainly, and also from religious teachings. We learn that we are defective or bad or

☙

even feel inferior (low self-worth). It all comes from our negative programming. Some professors have gone so far as to say it is an illness or even a disease if it becomes chronic or progressive.

What are the characteristics of a codependent? There are a vast number of answers to this question, too many to name, but let's review a few of them. Codependents try to please others instead of themselves and are often attracted to needy people. They may feel used, are bored and feel empty if they have no one to help. Often they overcommit themselves. Most codependents have fear of rejection and blame themselves for everything that goes wrong. They don't think they deserve good things in life and they desire love but settle for being needed. In addition they are worriers, can't get things done and lose sleep over problems. Codependency is a widespread problem, encompassing many people in all walks of life. Just look around you at how many people you know who fit into one or more of these categories. It affects the majority of our society to some degree and very often is a chronic way of living life. The sad part of this is that so many people deny there is a codependency problem or they ignore it by saying it'll be better tomorrow or that it's not really as bad as it seems. Often codependents stay busy so as not to think about the problem and become workaholics, or even get depressed and sick.

It also causes another problem: trying to control others. Codependents want things their way, afraid to let events happen naturally and get easily frustrated or angry. It could also be that they try to control someone by coercion or manipulation. This controlling is actually the main characteristic of a codependent person.

The controlling aspect rears its head so often in relationships, whether it be parent/child, husband/wife or between friends. At this point we can see how surrendering your will is a difficult maneuver for a codependent person. Giving up control is a frightening thing to these people because then they feel power-

❧

less and totally vulnerable. It can block God's power and definitely stunt their growth and then they lose themselves. When we are trying to control the impossible we often stop the possible from happening. Did you realize the full impact of that last statement? It means when we try to control people and events in our lives we often prevent the very thing from happening that we want to happen!

Codependency often prevents someone from getting close to another person and causes a great deal of vacillation with the emotions. They let someone hurt them and just keep bouncing back for more; at the same time they will actually protect and cover up for that person. How many times have we heard of a woman who stays in a relationship, hiding the fact that her partner beats her? This is a perfect example of codependency. Or maybe someone is married to an alcoholic and lies to prevent anyone knowing the truth. That in actuality cripples the alcoholic even more. It may cause various sexual problems as well. Maybe sex becomes a duty or it might be withheld in a manipulative play, or perhaps it is a means of holding on, basically controlling.

Why do people fall so easily into codependency? The core reason is that they don't love themselves. If you don't love yourself you can't love anyone else, neither will you feel worthy of love. Many times parental love is with conditions, so this feeling of being unloved is a basis for codependency. The daughter who becomes pregnant in her teen years and is sent away to have the baby or maybe never forgiven for the "shame" brought to the parents is a good example. Perhaps a son drops out of college and becomes a musician in a band, very happy doing what he loves but not creating the "dream" career of being a lawyer as dad wanted. Perhaps you married the wrong person according to your parents and they never got over it. That is love with condi-

❧

tions. As a result, people become codependent, looking for relationships to fill the void, seeking approval and even staying in relationships that aren't working because they feel that anything is better than nothing.

This was me. I felt trapped in an unworkable relationship and at the same time felt I didn't deserve anything better. I had allowed childhood programming to totally affect my adult decisions, fearing my ability to listen to my own spirit. That was codependency control. I kept thinking it would get better or that maybe it was my fault or that people would think badly of me for breaking up the family. All this resulted from allowing others to control my life, from parents to spouse to children to church to friends. But finally, when it felt like there was no way out, I saw that the prison door was open, the door that had been unlocked all the time, and I slowly walked toward the light and freedom; freedom for my soul to live!

Caretakers and/or rescuers are one of the most common types of codependents. They live their lives taking care of everyone but themselves. That gives credence to their life. The problem is that their spirit gets lost and often they become frustrated and angry without even being aware of why they are. Their life is on hold while they try to fix everyone else's. Caretaking can be a substitute for intimacy. Mothers and wives fall into this category many times, often feeling like martyrs, being overcommitted. This was my life! It was so good to be busy and nurturing and needed and loved. But wait, what kind of love was that? That was the typical controlling love: I take care of you in love and you respond in love. I never grew, though, so as the marriage fell apart and the children began to leave, the bottom fell out. At this point I began to see the reality of being a whole person on my own, able to love myself and others, with no judgment or conditions. If you feel that your stability and security is based on what someone does or

❧

doesn't do, then you have no stability at all. This was an eye-opener, but it took a while to learn!

Everyone must be able to be complete on their own and fulfill their own purpose. Without this completeness they will be codependent. Everyone wants love in their life, that special person to whom they are connected. Codependency doesn't allow that freedom while real love does. It allows one to be alone and be an individual, apart from the other, to trust and to actually encourage expansion. Without these qualities it won't work and, if these individuals stay together, it will be a prison. Codependents often can't live with someone, but feel they can't live without them either.

So how can one learn to be independent, shedding the codependency traits? First you become aware of this problem. Acknowledge you are codependent; that's the most important step. Then you must accept where you are. At that point you put yourself on the side of reality rather than fighting it. It is then that you begin to feel your own feelings and you're on the road to peace and healing.

The third step is assertive action, or taking control of you and your life. Your family may at first think you are selfish as you begin to think of yourself in new ways, but amazingly, most life situations are improved as we take care of ourselves. We must forgive ourselves for our past mistakes, and then recognize a job well done. We take time for ourselves to restore and value our own soul. Detach from other's lives and set boundaries. What do I need? What will enhance my life to bring my spirit to a new awareness of my goals in life? Listen to yourself!

Since your thoughts are a key to your feelings, take inventory of your thoughts every day. Those thoughts create your life, so often it will be necessary to change them. Feed your mind positive, healthy data and stretch your mind to unknown areas without limitations. This is how you grow and change into what you want to become. You alone can do this.

It is absolutely magical to set goals and write them down. When you do this it sets into motion a powerful psychological, spiritual and emotional force because it makes us aware of what we should be doing and need to accomplish. Then let go and let God. There are no limits to what you can do and be when you ask for God's help! Letting go means trusting His timing, and then patiently waiting. This is one of the hardest things to do, but the rewards make it worth every moment you wait!!!

It is only a tiny rosebud,
a flower of God's design;
but I cannot unfold the petals
with these clumsy hands of mine.

The secret of unfolding flowers
is not known to such as I;
God opens this flower so sweetly,
when in my hands they fade and die.

If I cannot unfold a rosebud,
this flower of God's design,
then how can I think I have wisdom
to unfold this life of mine?

So I'll trust in Him for His leading
each moment of every day;
I will look to him for His guidance
each step of the pilgrim way.

The pathway that lies before me,
only my Heavenly Father knows;
I'll trust Him to unfold the moments,
just as He unfolds the rose.

—AUTHOR UNKNOWN

CHAPTER 14

⸕

Letting Go

Change is hard but necessary for growth and there is no gain without pain.

I wondered what the first Christmas after my divorce would be like. How would it be as far as family traditions go. I decided to do many things the same in keeping traditions, but I also decided to start some new ideas. I kept the tradition of a nine foot tree and one son helped me put it in the house and one daughter helped me decorate it. There weren't as many presents under the tree but enough, and I had borrowed money to provide those gifts as it was. (I took care of that debt quickly). So far, so good. I was worried about being alone on Christmas Eve and Christmas night as my kids were to be with their dad, but I realized this was something I had to face so I literally turned it over to God and let go of it. Lo and behold my ex-husband received the gift of a stomach virus and I received the gift of my children with me. God does work in mysterious ways! Then it came time for Christmas morning. We opened our gifts the same way as always and had a good time. Dinner would be the same as before with mom spending two days in the kitchen preparing turkey, dressing, her rolls, pies etc., only to have it devoured in 20 minutes! But this year was to bring a surprise. Three of my children were at the dinner table with one friend and myself and after we ate we started talking. One of my children made a comment that remains embedded in my memory for all eternity when it was said: "This is the best Christmas I've ever had; it's peaceful." The others chimed in as well. It was all I could do to keep the tears from flowing, but I knew then all was well. We kept talking and then one child said: "We ought to celebrate with that champagne" (someone had given me a bottle). So I said: "Why not?" This was definitely a break from tradition for me, especially with minors involved, but then I thought, why not have fun; this *is* a celebration. We chilled it on ice for 30 minutes, but as the cork popped off it had a mind of its own, hit the ceiling hard and zoomed around the room, barely missing a head or two. We all cracked up until the tears flowed and we all toasted a wonderful traditional and non-traditional moment. We actually talked and laughed for over an hour before even beginning to clean up from dinner. I realized anew that I had made the perfect choice for this family in filing for that divorce. Everyone, including their dad, was so much better than before. Later, my daughters and I went to the movies, another break from tradition. Letting go and letting God work out the details always gives you blessings beyond anything you could have ever imagined.

Surrendering your own will is perhaps the most difficult feat in your life, but necessary in order to be happy and peaceful. Knowing that everything flows in divine order when you get out of the way, produces an inner serenity because all that comes into your life will be what is best for you. I was a master at control; I still fight it. All of my adult life I had tried to control my life and those involved in my life, without realizing that's what I was doing. I would punish my children because they were guilty of sins. That's how I had been taught. I was taught to fear my sinful nature and the punishment it would entail. Because I could never feel worthwhile due to those imperfections, I was always

✂

guilty and therefore never deserving of good things in my life. That was my mindset.

One of the times in my life in which I totally let go was in 1982 as it was nearing time for the birth of my fifth child. My husband refused to be part of the childbirth process, but I had wanted him to be part of it and coach me for a natural birth. He was not interested. Where we lived at this time required the viewing of a film and a class for the expectant dad to even be in the labor room, but after watching his reaction to the film I totally gave up on convincing him to help me and be with me. I had already had four babies alone so I could do it again. After about three hours of labor I was about to be taken to the delivery room (I was fortunate to have short labors) when a little "granny" nurse appeared and asked my husband why he wasn't suited up for the delivery. He answered he wasn't going in so she said, "Of course you are." They argued back and forth a few minutes and she said for him to hurry up or he would miss the entire event. To my utter disbelief he went into the next room, suited up and was in delivery with me. I can't say he was too excited about it - a little white in the face - but he was there. When you let go of a situation it always works out in the least expected way. It may not bring the result you asked for, but whatever the result it will be better than you had imagined.

The secret to letting go is to surrender the situation or problem completely and then make sure you don't take it back. This is where so many of us get into trouble; we give it to God but turn right around and take it back. If you are guilty of this - I can assure you everyone does this at one time or another - don't beat yourself up over it, just release it to God once again. Until you learn the lesson it will continually jump up and bite you in the face. As you continually do this it will become easier and easier to accomplish. In the previous example I had not only turned it over to God, but I had literally forgotten about it - after all there was

❦

no hope for me to get what I wanted! Then look what happened.

When you continually try to control your life, not getting your way can be very stressful and cause you a great deal of grief. This stress can have a snowball effect and literally reduce your life to an unhappy, anxiety-filled existence, more like going through the motions of life on a time-bomb. Sooner or later it will cause health problems because, according to many health advocates, our physical disorders are a direct result of emotional and/or spiritual imbalance. This is no way to live and certainly is not a fun way; this is not what God wants for our lives. He wants us happy and fulfilled, joyful from the inside out. There's a poem that a friend gave me several years ago and one that I in turn have repeatedly given to others. I keep it on the front of my refrigerator and on my bathroom mirror and it goes like this:

> *Good morning, this is God.*
> *I'm going to be handling all*
> *your problems today and*
> *I don't need your help,*
> *so enjoy your day!*
> —AUTHOR UNKNOWN

I think this poem illustrates all I've been saying throughout this book - give it to God and enjoy your life, celebrate it!

As I conclude this section about the lessons to be learned from life, rest assured there is a way to improve your life and erase these negative emotional tendencies that prevent you from living your life to the max. As you proceed into part III you will learn how to transform your life through various methods and avenues that can benefit all areas of your life and put you on a path to complete wholeness, the balancing of the mind, body and spirit. *Namaste!*

Metamorphosis

Now awaken sweet spirit
silently emerging from the shadows of time
no longer hidden from the world's eyes.
Share your beautiful soul
as you gracefully unfold your glorious wings
and flutter into the light magically free.

Dear God, guide me...

—CAROLYN PORTER

Preface

Metamorphosis means transformation or a complete change of character, appearance and form. Anyone who knew me a couple of years ago would tell you this depicts me. I am in no way, shape or form the same person physically, emotionally, mentally or spiritually that I was before, and all I can say is, "Thank you God for this incredible gift of transformation!"

I think of myself as the butterfly finally emerging from the cocoon. First there was the brown, fuzzy caterpillar, who crawled very slowly, quite limited in life experiences. Then came time to remain dormant, introspective, as changes slowly began to be manifested. The world couldn't see them; they were hidden from view in the shadow of the cocoon. Ever so slowly, with a great deal of effort, pain and courage, the transforming caterpillar began ripping apart the cocoon and out flew a beautiful, colorful butterfly. As she spread her graceful wings and fluttered up into the glittering light of the soft, blue sky, she was free. All the confinement was left behind as she shed her old life. At last she could experience the freedom to soar to heights she had never before known, to follow her own path with a sense of pure wonder, and to know her limitless possibilities if she just believed in miracles!

My dream is that each of you can experience this awakening. As you re-read the poem that preceded this preface, ask God to stir the spirit within you to know that this moment is that magical, perfect chance to begin anew!

BUTTERFLY

A man found a cocoon of a butterfly. After a while a small opening appeared. He sat and watched the butterfly for several hours as it struggled to force its small body through that little hole. Then it seemed to stop with any further progress. It appeared as if it had completely given out and could go no further. Feeling sorry for the butterfly, the man took a pair of scissors and clipped off the remaining part of the cocoon. The butterfly emerged easily but it had a swollen body and small, shriveled wings. The man continued to watch the butterfly because he expected that, at any moment, the wings would enlarge and expand to be able to support the body, which would contract in time. Neither happened! In fact, the butterfly spent the remainder of its life crawling around with a swollen body and shriveled wings. It never was able to fly. What the man did not understand, was that the restricting cocoon and the struggle required for the butterfly to get through the tiny opening were God's way of forcing fluid from the body of the butterfly into its wings so that it would be ready for flight, once it achieved its freedom from the cocoon. Oftentimes struggles are exactly what we need in our lives. If God allowed us to go through our lives without any obstacles, it would cripple us. We would never become as strong as what we could be.

—AUTHOR UNKNOWN

To release the past and begin anew
take one step out in faith,
God guides your journey
as healing flows through your soul.
The tears come and go
as the sun peaks through the glistening rainbow.

—CAROLYN PORTER

⤸

CHAPTER 15

Peeling Away the Layers

The preceding story illustrates this chapter so perfectly. Peeling away the layers of past hurts, anger, fear, shame and all the other negatives in our lives is often a slow and painful process, but this is our gift. Every time a crisis occurs we either succumb to the weight of it or we rise above it and grow stronger. God *never* gives us more than we can handle, but it is only in overcoming these obstacles that our lives are transformed and we can fly free.

Envision an onion. It has many layers and, as one layer is removed, another is revealed. There are tears as each layer is discarded for a new one. Finally you've reached the core. This is how healing occurs, one step at a time. As you peel away each layer you begin the rebirthing of your spirit; you're at the center of your being.

Peeling away the layers was difficult for me as it always is, but every discarded layer is a triumph that echoes singing in heaven. Each layer that is removed puts you one step closer to being a whole person who is able to care for yourself. This often is a painful process but is one of the most precious gifts you'll ever receive. This is how you grow and expand and unveil your soul. Always remember there's a rainbow right behind the storm clouds.

❧

Changes occur in our lives continuously. First there is kindergarten when we leave mom, and then graduation from high school might take us far from home. Then perhaps marriage and children, who in turn leave, causing yet another variation in our lives. There could be job changes, residence moves or even marital changes; these are natural occurrences we encounter as human beings on this earth. But the alterations, the peeling away of the layers I'm talking about, really have less to do with our physical being and more to do with our emotional and spiritual components. We are three-dimensional beings, composed of body, mind and spirit, and all three must be addressed in order to be a complete person. Our physical life is actually created by our emotional and spiritual dimension and our thoughts create our words and our actions. It took me a very long time for this enlightenment.

Throughout my teen years and into young adulthood I had a lot of questions concerning religious beliefs as well as where my life was going. All I could think of was to get married, have babies, and do something to bring in money. I loved being a mom and running a household, I was good in this role, but in hindsight I realize I always had to be creating something. I was never satisfied with anything I accomplished. I was continually on to something more, another creation. I often felt restless, searching, but for what I didn't know. No matter what I did I didn't think it was enough, and yet I was frequently told I accomplished a great deal. There was a deep yearning inside my heart for something greater and I really began to sense this as my first child reached adulthood. What would happen when they were all gone? What would I do with my life? You see, I was missing the whole point of my existence. Perhaps you are thinking right now that this sounds like you. You aren't sure who you are or what your life is about. Is life just to find a mate, raise children, make money, have fun, move into retirement and finally leave this earth? Not exactly. Each of us has a purpose to fulfill while in this existence, a gift to use in serving and loving God and our fellow men. But many people move aimlessly through their journey, their purpose totally obscured from view, therefore missing the point of life itself!

I was at this very place when things began to fall apart for me in my life. I was so unhappy, expecting others to make me happy, not realizing I was responsible for my own happiness. The restlessness became stronger and stronger and then God intervened.

I believe the turning point in my life began when the homeopathic doctor gave me a remedy that forced all the suppressed hurts and anger to begin surfacing, which in turn forced me to begin my journey into finding who I am. It began with following a physical path and, although it could never complete the process, it was important to the process. Many might say this was just a coincidence, but there are no coincidences! It was simply God sending a miracle into my life.

I shared in earlier chapters some of the problems I had physically as a result of these buried feelings. These feelings were very much alive, as was evident from my reaction to that remedy. You may bury your emotions, but they never die, as Karol Truman reiterates in her book entitled *Feelings Buried Alive Never Die*. Every cell in your body has a memory, and it remembers every negative emotion you've ever felt - all the resentment, anger, fear, bitterness, and rejection that you hid when it was manifested in you. Many people in alternative health care state that all illness is emotionally based, that we actually create it in our lives by our own negative emotions and thoughts. This occurs because it alters our chemical balance, which allows changes at a cellular level. It's important to learn to surrender and release your anger and resentment and then replace it with positive emotions like love and forgiveness.

As I sought the path that would bring healing to my body, I tried many alternative remedies. I had given up totally on traditional medical treatment because it had only covered up my ailments with drugs. I discovered at the library the answer to the candida problem which involved eliminating sugar, dairy, yeast and gluten grains from my diet. It felt like I had little left to eat but I soon realized that it was the good things that were left! I worked with herbal remedies, too, and certainly improved my health for a few years. But when I took the homeopathic remedy all hell broke loose and I began what seemed a downward spiral. It felt that way because many layers of emotions had surfaced at once and the anxiety was unbearable. Everything bothered me. My heart raced, my insides were shaky and my legs weak, so that I rarely went anywhere alone, fearing I wouldn't make it. But I did make it and over the next few years I tried one thing after another, from herbal remedies to vitamin supplements, to various nutritional diets, relaxation techniques, massage, chiropractic adjustments, kinesiology, Reike and so forth. The terrible anxiety began to fade and although I improved I couldn't remain there; I wasn't well yet. I read continuously and did discover a lot of things to help myself and my customers, but it was hard to figure out which program was correct with so many different choices. Every book I read said it had the answer but how could they all be right? That's when I really became aware of the other aspects of my being and started searching for answers through emotional and spiritual work. As I mentioned before, it takes a balance of body, mind and spirit to be healthy and complete. I'm not undermining the physical approach to health because it is definitely a necessary part, but until I rectified the emotional and spiritual dilemmas in my life I couldn't remain well. Thus my journey proceeded into the emotional and spiritual realm.

I mentioned going to an intuitive as being a very big early step in the right direction. I saw there was more to the physical exis-

ॐ

tence than I realized. It was quite a positive experience towards building my self-worth and understanding my potentials. I worked with brain gym and Reike and various people who implemented energy work, and I always got better for a brief while. I tried homeopathics which kept me in turmoil for two years until I discovered I couldn't handle them. A psychologist and counselor were utilized as well, all to the tune of a great deal of money. These measures improved my state, without a doubt, but there was still much work to be done.

The health stores my son and I opened were successful and thriving and they brought me into another area in which I could acquire some expertise. It was fun to be a store owner but after a while I noticed it was interacting with the people - customers, reps, delivery folks - that I loved the most. If someone came in and thanked me for helping them with a problem it would keep me high all day. I had been writing the newsletters for the stores and often customers would tell me how much they enjoyed them, some even saving them all. Things were developing of which I had no idea. Doors were about to open that would surprise and challenge me.

In September, 1998, I attended the seminar *Breaking The Money Barriers* that Dr. Michael J. Duckett presented. This I discussed in an earlier chapter but have to mention it again because of the significant role it played in my metamorphosis. It was time, I was ready. The things lacking in my life were brought out during the seminar, but in addition, it was obvious that Dr. Duckett lived what he taught. He touched on every aspect of life in a way I'd never heard before and I wanted a life like that. What was missing in my life was purpose. I didn't know the direction in which my life was headed. I wanted to be happy and fulfilled and I learned how to achieve that - by living on purpose and serving people, in love. Later I discovered that my purpose became my life! I can still remember how I felt that day as I left the seminar, in awe of what I had heard. I was scared; I would have to make a lot of changes in myself as well as my life. I couldn't remove the seminar from my thoughts so I began to utilize what I'd learned; I read my notes over and over. I worked on my fears and my negativity and things started to happen. Perhaps the single most striking thought that was presented was that problems are nothing more than an opportunity for growth. I had always felt them as heavy burdens, but this way of viewing an obstacle took away the negativity and the weight. I became happier in spite of all I was facing and life took on a new dimension.

The first step of change was the hardest, it always is, but with each step it became easier and easier. I also realized I had to take a giant step in faith and begin the divorce proceedings. The marriage was never going to work and I needed to move ahead with my life and find out who I was.

I began changing a great deal spiritually. I was reading many books on this subject and was fascinated by it. I had been religious all my life, but as I became more spiritual I found a depth of communion with God I'd not known before. I learned I was responsible for my life, no one else, and that God and my angels were with me constantly, guiding my steps. I was developing a new realm of consciousness, a new level of awareness of my being.

The emotional upheaval I experienced during this period as I peeled away so many layers seemed to be never-ending. I spent so many hours in tears and I would tell God I couldn't take this anymore. Sometimes I'd ask, "Where are you God? Are you listening to my pleas because this is hard?" He would always answer by saying that He'd never give me more than I could handle and that all of this was part of my process in becoming whole and free. I was growing! With every discarded layer came a greater sense of confidence that I could make it through whatever came my way.

There had been many buried layers over the years and each one began surfacing. There were deep psychological scars that went back to childhood. They involved such feelings as rejection, low self-esteem, insecurity, not feeling I deserved good things, anger and resentment. I felt a deep sadness that so many years had been spent in all this negative state. But I kept reminding myself, or my friends would remind me, that this was all divine timing.

It's very important to have supportive friends as you experience this release; they can help to ease the pain and be there for support. I was blessed with many wonderful friends who listened and prayed and were there for me. Sometimes I thought my heart would break, but my dearest friend, Deanna, would be there and help me through whatever came. We often walked together and would talk and I'd always feel better. While it is important to have these earth angels, I became aware that only I could do the work, that only I could release the negative thoughts and replace them with positive ones.

I had begun to meditate and pray every morning and evening for 20 minutes or so and I found this to be invaluable. God would speak to me as I quietly surrendered to Him and asked for guidance. I felt God's presence in a way I'd never experienced before. He wasn't a distant God up in heaven, but was part of me and every aspect of my life. My heart chakra opened up and love began to pour out, which erased the previous negative patterns. As I replaced fear with love I found myself doing things I'd never done before, things that were totally out of my comfort zone. Life was rapidly changing but there was a great deal of work yet to be accomplished.

As you bring past negative issues up into your conscious mind, you often experience physical symptoms until they are let go. They can be short-lived or can hang around a while, depending on the speed of your release. They can range from minor ailments

⚜

that are mainly an inconvenience to a debilitating illness that can keep you from functioning in a normal, everyday capacity. I fluctuated from light to severe and was able to push myself into functioning, but in the process I was causing adrenal exhaustion. This problem usually takes a long time to repair. Your adrenals are your stress gland and help to keep your stress level balanced.

I remember that I had to frequently pace, even while talking on the phone I couldn't sit still. I hated that wired feeling, the restlessness. You might find me walking in my yard at 3 a.m. because I couldn't sleep. Of course sleep is what I needed the most but it was difficult to obtain.

Once as I was en route to a practitioner's office I felt very confined, even though I was driving my large conversion van with lots of space. I literally didn't think I'd be able to continue on the expressway with cars on either side of me. It felt as if my van was closing in on me. I was trembling from head to toe accompanied by dry mouth, sweating and a feeling of not being able to breathe. All I wanted to do was pull over, jump out and either run or scream. It seemed I was out of control, in the midst of a panic attack. I kept praying and somehow I made it to the practitioners office, only to find out I would have to wait. I couldn't sit there so I went into the hall and just paced until it was my time. He worked with me and calmed me down for then. This was not fun, the anxiety was frightening and was my most debilitating symptom for a short period of time.

The physical symptoms of negative emotions can be many and varied. Some of the most common complaints from my customers and myself were fatigue, nervousness, anxiety, insomnia, depression, headaches, digestion problems, constipation/diarrhea, skin problems, lost interest in life, shaking, hair problems and so on. If the negative emotions are not discarded they will continue to manifest themselves and probably add new symptoms, worsening as time goes by. Disease always has an emotional root. Remember one example I gave earlier in the book that depression always has anger at the base. Thus it is with all disease. So in order to live a great, happy life with less disease, one must allow the release of bottled up injustices. I hadn't learned to do this yet but was in the process.

There are many paths you can choose to accomplish this healing; I've mentioned a few I implemented. Ask friends, health stores or whomever you trust for referrals to contact. Make sure that the person who gives you the referral is satisfied with his/her own improvement before you spend your money. If the practitioner you try doesn't work after a short while, keep looking until you find someone who works for you. I tried to remember how many different chiropractors, kinesiologists, naturopaths, nutritionists, medical doctors and others I utilized before I found the ones who could really help me, and I'd guess it was in the neighborhood of 25 different healthcare practitioners. Some gave no help at all and I quickly found others, while some offered a little assistance, but none ever rectified my entire health troubles. The reason for that was because I had to address the emotional and spiritual issues and cast them away and, until then, I couldn't be healed.

As I look back on all the suffering and the tears, and even the times I wondered if I'd ever be okay, I understand that God had given me a priceless gift. I certainly didn't think so as I was living through it; in fact I wasn't aware it was a gift. But through it all I acquired a great deal of knowledge about natural health and healing and thus have been able to help many people. That wasn't all. I found who I am and what I am to do with my life, which guided me in new directions that I'd have never known without enduring all I did. You see, all of this was important so I could be used in certain capacities that wouldn't have been accomplished without those particular experiences. The same could be true for you. Whatever you face is part of your plan.

✂

As layers dropped away my health improved, but mostly my attitude improved. I became more self-assured because I had taken control of my life and was expanding. There were many more areas to address but I also see now that there always will be parts of me that must grow. We are continually evolving throughout our lives, shedding one part of the cocoon at a time. Becoming single after thirty-two years of attachment had to be the most difficult obstacle I ever faced. I was petrified but I knew I had to do it. This was fear in the truest sense of the word, but as I took the steps and went into action the fear subsided. I had been codependent all of my life and always had someone who took care of me. Would I be able to live on my own?

This very fact of codependency keeps many women in unhappy, deteriorating marriages that are devouring them and destroying their spirit. Sometimes it's the financial dependency that is the big factor in the decision to remain. It has long been documented that it's harder for a woman to earn the same salary as a man of equal ability or level, so the fear of enough income can be somewhat justified. I had to face both of these issues and it wasn't easy to do. I really wasn't sure how I would accomplish all I had to do but I knew I would. You see, it's all in the timing. This is such an important statement that I feel it warrants repetition. I had been to Dr. Duckett's seminar and was opening up to the spiritual part of me so that my entire perspective of life had shifted. I was now ready to take this major step even though I couldn't see how I'd manage. Once I made the decision, however, there was no looking back. I had a goal to achieve and I would do it. That's the way all of life should be. Once you set your eyes on your goal, never take your eyes away from that goal. Know in your heart you will accomplish it. When you do this you are successful. As the obstacles bump into you, you'll steady yourself and keep right on trucking.

It doesn't mean you won't have many moments of weakness and sadness. I had so many I couldn't count them all. It wasn't that I ever wanted to go back either. I wanted to be loved and connected to someone, sharing with him and giving. I also wanted to be desired. The feeling of not being wanted, this rejection, is a difficult pill to swallow. It certainly undermines your self-esteem and it crushes your ego to know the person who was to cherish you couldn't and wouldn't and really hadn't for a very long time. It's lonely by yourself and quite a feeling of uncertainty surfaces. But what was happening to me was the greatest gift I would ever receive. I was finally growing up. The real me was being unveiled. The seed that had been planted was finally sprouting. I had uprooted myself from everything familiar and comfortable, my home, my dependence, my career, my finances, and my religion. I was still in the cocoon but a large crack had appeared. Just like the butterfly exhaustingly struggles to free herself from the confinement of the cocoon, so does every woman who undertakes executing her freedom. This applies to anyone searching for her own self and it doesn't mean a divorce is the way to freedom. Freedom means claiming your soul and shedding the cocoon after the transition of your being. The transition requires many stages, none of which can be skipped.

There are still layers to shed, there always will be. The scales have tipped so that the negativity is way at the bottom. What a difference it makes when this shift occurs. As things surface for me today, they seem to be less severe and of shorter duration, or is it that I am aware of what is happening and how to handle it? The first words I utter as situations arise are "Thank you God for this gift." It's another chance for growth and blessings, and remember, God always knows what's best for you.

The most important part of healing is forgiveness. When you learn to forgive you release your own power, and you love uncon-

❦

ditionally. The key to happiness and contentment in this life is to love no matter what. This love is not judgmental. It doesn't mean you have to allow yourself to be subjected to the negative response of a particular person, you just forgive that person. You may need to detach yourself from that person, as I did in divorcing, but if you recall my healing really progressed as I forgave my former husband. Forgiveness releases the past and allows the hurts to be lifted away. Imagine the angels carrying them far away out of your view.

Of equal importance is forgiving yourself. You've made mistakes, we all have, but forgive them and let the guilt go. You will notice your body feels lighter and there will be a spring in your step. It is then you will become an authentically empowered woman!

The people who come into your life and push your buttons the most are your greatest teachers. I have a printed saying in my office that states much to me and it goes like this "When the student is ready the teacher appears." Through them you learn your greatest lessons!

Real love lies beyond what mind doth know
piercing to depths these beloved souls,
unveiling the wounds, then letting them go;
strength and power unmasked, magically transforming
love gives and grows with joy unknown,
healing the spirits, forever entwined
through loving eyes to be truly seen.
In ecstasy these hearts unite,
on eagles wings do soar;
God's gift so sweet, reflecting our dreams,
the enchantment of paradise with your hand in mine.

—CAROLYN PORTER

CHAPTER 16

❧

Love Beyond Words

Everyone wants to love and be loved; it's one of man's deepest desires. But so many people have no idea how to accomplish this. Society thinks of love as a strong, warm feeling towards another, affection or a zap of chemistry. Its viewpoint involves sharing interests, enjoying togetherness, and sexual passion. This is a physical expression of love, infatuation, but can it stand the test of time? Love as this is an illusion because you can't stay there!

Real love expands way beyond the physical. It exists in a different realm of consciousness than is portrayed in earthly lives. It penetrates the soul and seeks to find who two people really are. It is love without judgement, totally unconditional, a spiritual connection.

Boy meets girl and a spark flies. The dating process begins and before long, for most partners, their love gravitates them to the bedroom. Physical chemistry is strong and this is what most people call love. Perhaps they built a friendship first but many ignore that and go straight to the physical. The problem is that without a deep spiritual connection the likelihood of the relationship surviving is much reduced. Look at the divorce rate and it's easy to see what kind of love most people have. It's very superficial so that as problems and personality differences appear couples can't

❧

handle it. Many who brave the storms and stay together are very unhappy. I have met so many retired people who can't stand being together but can't bear to be alone. They just tolerate each other. I've heard many in their 60s or even earlier say it's too late now and have resigned themselves to a continuing life of misery. They are prisoners!

People in this situation are allowing concepts and other people to control their life in a detrimental way. They aren't being true to themselves. It's also another example of codependency. No one should stay in a destructive, non-nurturing relationship because they feel there is no way out, that they are chained. Although I fully believe in miracles, the majority of the time relationships like this continue to deteriorate and more anger and resentment builds. Of course I do believe in working on a relationship. I participated in counseling either by myself or with my former husband several times, but it wasn't meant to work. If one partner grows and the other doesn't want to, it is time to leave. As I began changing and growing the path divided completely. In hindsight, I think I knew this early on. But remember the saying: Love is blind; blind that is 'til you turn on the light.

Another common downfall of two people is the "need" for each other. They feel they need that person to complete them or make them feel better or just take care of them. Think of someone who procures a divorce, such as myself. The first thing I wanted to do was find someone else. That's codependency. We think we need a partner to fill the void in our lives, not realizing the void lies within ourselves. Rushing into another relationship soon after dissolving a partnership spells trouble. There hasn't been time for healing or letting go and that person will then attract the same kind of person they just let go. This is evident over and over in life situations. Someone marries an abuser, divorces, and then picks the same type person who perhaps displays another branch of abuse. God had other plans for me, namely to be on my own for a while and release and heal. I began to find out who I am. You can want someone but you must be a complete person, standing in your own power. There are many steps to accomplish this feat and many tears will be shed, but it is worth the effort. Then the relationship you establish will be deep and masterful and a love like none you've ever known.

Let's talk about real love. If your spouse still sends tingles up and down your spine after 30 years of marriage, you have definitely achieved more than most do. But it must go deeper than even that. True love must be open and free in order to work. This means there must be complete trust and lack of judgement. A partner who is jealous or possessive is not trusting. In so many marriages or relationships a partner, particularly a man, feels as if he's on a leash, or maybe the wife/mother feels she's a slave to her family. Each person should have his/her own time, and be able to be with friends or pursue separate interests without pangs of guilt. It's important to follow some of your own dreams and not be attached at the hip to your mate. Space gives you room to breathe and gives a new sense of appreciation and love for your partner.

Real love must give room to bloom and expand. In my own marriage I was feeling stifled and stuck, wondering where my life was going. I thought about how life would be without kids. I had no idea who I really was. But circumstances forced me to take inventory and question my direction.

Growth is change and usually brings pain. There's a saying that without pain there is no gain. This pain, however, is a blessing from God that will make you stronger and uncover your soul. Marianne Williamson says in *Enchanted Love*, that real love is not comfortable at all and in fact pushes every button and challenges every strength. It also brings up weaknesses and wounds to heal. The purpose of spiritual love is to pierce the armor that hides the heart, letting the heart break, then allowing it to heal the hurts and soar to heights unknown. Each person in this kind of relationship stretches their heart and requires the establishment of separate identities, each strong alone, and then a deep and powerful relationship ensues. This love transforms each partner.

Being a person in your own right is often very difficult for a woman, even in this liberated time. Traditionally raised women are programmed to believe they are partners with a man but subservient. Although we are making a momentous shift in this millennium to create a different scenario for women, many were taught a mindset of submissiveness and have trouble eradicating it. It stems primarily from the church and religious teachings. This was the patriarchal viewpoint prevalent at that time, but we don't live in the "olden days" any more. It was customary for men and women to eat separately and walk separately, but that system is over. So why continue the subservient mindset? It is outdated. We are living in a new age that is unfolding big changes in the concept of relationships, shifting to equal partners, each a whole person who can stand alone. Along with that thought pattern, there is a requirement for each person to find his/her mission in life and pursue it. It is then and only then that you will be happy and fulfilled and can contribute to a beautiful relationship.

Real enchanted love brings up wounds to heal. It is one of the gifts of such love. As each person feels the freedom to unveil emotions, new depths are reached in the relationship. The deepest fears emerge and it is only at that time that healing can take place. You must expose the darkness, those ugly, festering hurts, to break free and be whole. That is the purpose of a loving, intimate relationship - to reveal the weaknesses and just let them go, loving unconditionally. Then each can be truly seen and restored.

A true intimate relationship must allow distancing. After being close one needs to restore his/her own individuality. Staying in a

⌘

permanent state of closeness is not desirable because you lose your sense of balance and who you are, and you can't get anything done. Many of you have read *Men Are From Mars, Women Are From Venus* by John Gray, and he mentions that men often need to retreat into their cave and work out a situation. A woman who truly loves a man has no problem with this behavior. In fact she can use that time to re-focus herself, knowing that he'll be back. He further states it is like the man is stretching out a rubber band, but he can only go so far before coming back to you better than ever. Without allowing this freedom and space in a relationship, a great many hurts and resentments begin to build, usually stuffed away and buried, but very much alive. Distancing time is vital to any healthy, intimate relationship!

More and more people are looking for a spiritual partnership. In a spiritual partnership one partner creates the opportunity for growth in the other. The old model of marriage isn't working. Couples want more depth and expansion. They are following their hearts. These partners are on a spiritual journey, one that is formed for spiritual growth. The development of each soul is the most important thing, even more important than their relationship with each other. People have discovered that shallow talk isn't enough any longer, nor is just making money, raising children, buying houses or playing tennis. They long for depth and understanding and being appreciated as an individual first and foremost. We're even seeing marriage vows changing. Tradition isn't acceptable so much any more; couples are writing their own special words that mean something to them and indicate the new desire for profundity and connection. When partners help each other grow they are aligning their soul with their personality, which then makes them aware of all the possibilities they have as a creative being. This is personal empowerment, when each individual can expand to new planes and unfold his/her potential. This is true freedom.

✂

In a committed partnership it is vital to be truthful to each other and express all feelings, even anger. This is part of the process, the steps involved in building. Stating that you are angry is necessary in relaying inner emotions whereas raving outbursts aren't. To tell your partner you're angry at something he/she did to you is healthy verbalizing that keeps you from stuffing it into the resentment file. Communication is at the core of relationships, especially conveying your true thoughts. So often one partner, or both, keep silent and bury layer upon layer of hurts that build into a mountain over time. Eventually the volcano erupts, one way or another, and the partnership will dissipate. You might even remain together in the same house, but the wall gets higher and thicker to the point that nothing will penetrate it.

Love is the essence of our being, our hearts crave it. But you must love yourself first. If you don't love and accept yourself it will be impossible to love another. This lack of self-love stems from low self-worth that is prevalent in so many people. God created us and He would not create something that wasn't of value. Furthermore, we're all part of God and God is love. God loves us without reservation, just as we are with our mistakes. So our first step towards building a solid connection is loving ourselves as God loves us. Once we know our value we can in turn give to others and love flows from us abundantly. It's hard for a lot of people to accept themselves as they are but it's the most important step down the path to real love. After all, our relationships are simply a barometer of who we are. We are powerful, vibrational beings. Remember the law of cause and effect: what you give out comes back to you. We only have what we give away!

Giving is the true nature of genuine love. Enchanted love gives, then gives some more and keeps right on giving with no thought for what will come back. It's not part of the equation.

Most relationships are about what "I" get with many strings attached. Did he forget to call about being late or forget your birthday or is he withdrawn now and you want his time? You're mad because he forgot to pick up the ice for the party that starts shortly at your house and he's late on top of that, so wasn't able to help in the preparations. You perceived a certain way he should act and as a result you give him the cold shoulder all evening, shooting daggers with your eyes and then tell him to sleep on the sofa. Sound familiar? Real love means in spite of, but it can be tough to do. Often couples keep a running tab of how much one does in comparison with the other, making sure the columns stay even. Actually, when you expect nothing in return and just keep loving and giving, it comes back to you many times over. Selfless love such as this is beyond the comprehension of many, but this is an enduring, continuous flow of giving. Love such as this reaches past the normal realm of consciousness and becomes mystical and spiritual, not seen through earthly eyes.

Spiritual love exhibits forgiveness; in fact it's the cornerstone of a healthy love. Abandon the judgments and preconceived ideas of what should be and just allow love to flow. Forgiveness sets the scene for love to flourish.

Sometimes a spiritual love fades away. One partner continues to expand but the other is content to remain as he/she is. The lessons have been learned so the reason for the relationship is over; healing is complete. Forgiving allows you to leave easier and in peace. Even though the partnership dissolves, the connection will never end. To stay in this relationship would grasp the spirit of the growing partner and choke the life out of that person. Release and let go. To remain would be the sad, slow dance of death.

Falling in love when it's deep and spiritual is magnificent. When two souls genuinely combine spiritual forces they actually

❦

generate the power of God. These partners know they are together to grow spiritually. This internal love is not physical and can exist on it's own. If, however, physical love has a spiritual connection first, it is a gift that knows no limits! Real love magically transforms each soul reflecting the enchantment of paradise.

The mighty oak so strong
reaching towards the sky
as dew glistens on each leaf.
Majestic it stands in silence,
a master in time.
Its power known to all who see.
A tiny acorn was once this tree,
a miracle from God's own hand.

—CAROLYN PORTER

CHAPTER 17

∞

Emerging

The cocoon is full of shadows, a dull film coats the sides, blocking the sun. But as I emerged, wiping the slumber from my eyes, I was blinded by the brightness of the light as it illuminated the gift of life. So long confined and held back was my experience of an existence much like a dormant caterpillar. In order to enjoy the thrilling light of day you must first taste the darkness of night. Only as your eyes grow accustomed to the brightness can you know the majestic manifestation of beauty as it pierces the depths of your soul. My wings began to unfold and as I opened them full-spread I knew I was finally alive. It was time to explore this new realm and see the world as it really is - full of wonder and excitement. I slowly fluttered my wings and timidly ascended into the heavens, as my wide-open eyes beheld the earth below. Flitting from flower to flower and leaf to leaf, I experienced an expansion with the unfolding of each new mystery. A gift it was when one wakes up to life, as a child on Christmas morning stands with awe and wonderment as he sees the colorful array of packages beneath the glittering tree. Having traveled both paths, my soul chooses to fly free.

When I think about my life before the surge of expansion I think of a light that is hidden by a dense tree. When you look

∽

from just the right angle you can see a flicker of light peeking between the branches. It reminds me of a song I used to sing when a child called This Little Light of Mine. The words say to let your light shine for the world to see instead of hiding it. Hopefully if you are hiding your light, you are ready to bring it forth and let it shine brightly.

Emerging is the final stage in transforming. Transforming is made manifest with the ensuing changes, all part of the step by step process. Emerging brings into view all the new miraculous transitions of your soul for the whole world to envision. This is the method of becoming true to yourself instead of hiding behind other people and their teachings. You have established your unique individuality, no longer adhering to the beliefs of any other thought.

As you have read my account you have discovered that the changes were something which required taking one step at a time. You can't rush the steps nor can you skip any of them. You might try to take matters into your own hands and force something into reality by attempting control, but you always lose.

When you have become the butterfly you have completed a feat worthy of recognition. No longer are you concerned what others think. Your feet are firmly planted on the ground, your legs are strong, your head held high and you smile as your eyes focus on the world. You walk straight and tall, ready to fulfill your mission in life as the angels gently encircle you with their wings. Obstacles are thrown at you, so you duck and keep moving. You have learned some very important lessons but you've learned how to let your light shine in all situations.

There is such a freedom after leaving the cocoon. Every day, all through the day, I thank God for all the challenges that come my way, because that's how I grow. Then I let go of the struggles and give them back to God. What release that is!! Challenges will continue to block your path, but the freedom comes when you let go and give them back to your Creator.

All my life I had hidden behind programmed patterns and thoughts of others. I really had no identity of my own. I was always trying to fit into the mold provided for me, but I never could fit. I was afraid to venture out on my own. If you live like this you are not being true to yourself. Many people live their entire life through other people and their thoughts, fitting into the mold they pour for you. It doesn't take much thinking to exist in this form. I am thankful that my life is completely different than what I had imagined, and that a great restlessness in me eventually caused enough struggle that I could crack open the cocoon.

As the crack became larger and I looked out to see what was in the universe, I became anxious to break free completely. I asked God to open a door for me. He obliged, and I thought I knew what door it would be. But He surprised me, taking me totally out of my comfort zone! I know one thing for sure, don't ask God to direct your life and open doors unless you're ready to accept whatever comes your way; it may amaze you! I still marvel at the doors He has opened already and is continually opening. I can assure you that public speaking was the last thing I would have ever selected as one of my callings!

Fear is the biggest barrier that affects the opening of new doors. We sabotoge our minds by saying we can't accomplish these different adventures. God doesn't open these doors for us unless we can walk through them and have victory. The choice is ours, of course; we have free will. But one thing I have now learned is to never say no to God. If He opens a door I walk through it no matter what. Sometimes my knees buckle and my legs feel weak, but every time I say, "It's up to you God," it works!

Many changes have occurred in my priorities. I was an avid shopper and quite good at it. Now I rarely shop, purchasing

❀

mainly the needs on my list. I actually save much money this way and hours of time. I never did need all that I thought I needed anyhow.

I used to watch movies on TV in the evenings or on the weekends and enjoyed them. In the last two years I haven't watched more than a few hours of TV collectively. I'd rather read, write, exercise or communicate with my children and friends, all means of emotional, intellectual and spiritual expansion. I used to hate to be quiet - now I relish it.

The phone used to be a great companion as I talked to friends for long periods of time. Friends are wonderful treasures and I enjoy them often, but with shorter conversations for the most part. Most can be shared in much less time.

I spent hours creating elaborate culinary delights and a lot of it wasn't very healthy, as I incorporated sugar, dairy and white flour in them. Now I prefer simple food, lots of salads and raw vegetables. I still create many dishes but most are very health oriented and require much less time to prepare. I've managed to please the majority of people as I slowly convert them to healthier eating choices.

I'm not saying that the above mentioned things are wrong, but they consumed so much of my life before, causing me to waste a lot of time and money. Now my desire is my purpose—to help people make positive changes in their life. My life is dedicated to serving others with God's help, in love. In doing this I have found the meaning of true peace and happiness. Giving is what life is all about, and as we give to others God bestows blessings on us beyond what we can imagine. It's the ripple effect. Throw a pebble in a pond and watch the ripples slowly travel to the other bank. What you may not know is that the ripples come back to where you are underneath the surface. What you give is what you receive. Make sure you give from your heart in love.

✂

As this chapter concludes, I want to paint a clear picture of what I mean by emerging. This is the final step of transformation. It is the time when you step out into the light for the world to see your true soul. There is no more hiding in the shadows or behind the trees. You are free to be who you want to be. The shackles are removed. The cocoon has fallen away. The barrier of fear has broken down. You are free to pursue your dreams. Nothing limits you any longer. This does not mean you need a divorce to accomplish this, although it may be necessary for you. It only means you are to be a complete person in your own right, fully capable of walking your own spiritual journey, with or without a partner. This is a truly emerged, empowered woman whose capabilities are limitless!

You might believe the metamorphosis had reached completion, but it actually never is finalized in this life. If you stop changing you stop growing. Our lives should be in a continuous state of upgrading. You reach a certain plane, a goal you've set, but do you remain there? No, you set another goal and then another, because every goal you achieve places a desire in your heart for growing more. Next year, next month or even tomorrow you want to be better than you are today. This is upgrading and the gift is in the process. It's exciting to watch it all unravel. You long for something, maybe a dream trip to the Grand Cayman Islands. You plan it carefully, counting the days. Finally it's here and you enjoy every minute of it. But it's over so fast. It was the anticipation of that trip that helped you work towards your goal of actually experiencing it. Once you've experienced it, you begin thinking of something else to replace that dream. This is the never-ending process of growth and expansion.

As I emerged into a new dimension of consciousness, I realized that I had spent my entire time until then allowing life to happen to me. I had accepted what came my way as being what was supposed to be. Now I had to picture what I desired my life to be and desire to achieve it, after which I must set my goals and take the steps necessary to activate my dreams.

There are four basic steps for this process according to author and speaker Wayne Dyer. First you wish for something. Wishing is just a nice thought. Someone might comment that your home is beautiful and they wish they could have one like it. That's a simple thought that passes through your mind rather quickly. But the next step puts feeling into the equation and that is desire. Desire begins to make it feel real. You long for it and the interest begins to invade your thoughts — you want it. Belief is the third step. Now you're stating that this could become a reality. You can really purchase a house like you want because you actually desire it. You are now obtaining confidence in your dream manifesting. You start to research aspects involved in buying a house like that, how much you can afford, what you can do to increase your purchasing capabilities, etc. etc. Now your faith gets involved and you're believing that your wish can come true. This turns into passion, a knowing that it is real. In this step there is absolutely no doubt that you will achieve this goal. It's a sure thing. This is what happens when you *know* you are living your purpose. It actually becomes part of your vibrational beingness and you are so secure in this that no one or nothing can shake your steadfastness in reaching this objective. You have an intention and it is truth.

The hardest thing, but yet the most important part, is turning it over to God, taking your hands off so that He can work out the details. Once you master this, your life will flow together in unbelievable continuity. It is often the most difficult thing to accomplish.

As I close this chapter, I want to relate a story that Dr. Duckett told at one of his seminars that basically sums up this section and my entire book for that matter.

A man was watching a sports game on TV one evening, and his young daughter was playing in the area, but kept running in front of the TV and blocking his view. Several times he asked her to please move out of the way, but somehow she always seemed to end up in front of the TV. He noticed a picture of the world in a nearby newspaper so the idea struck him to cut the world up into small pieces and tell her to show how smart she was by putting it back together with tape. She liked the idea, so he settled back into his chair, feeling good about successfully occupying his daughter so that he could enjoy the program. To his amazement his daughter brought him the picture completely taped together in only ten minutes time. He asked her how she did this so fast to which she replied, "Oh that was easy daddy, the back of the world was a lady in a pretty dress, so I just put the lady together and the world got back together."

My message to you is, when the lady gets back together then the world gets back together. Each one of you makes a difference on our planet. Find your purpose, make it happen, and give YOU to the world!

Are we not dynamic beings
waiting to unfold,
God will always do the work
with miracles untold.

We know what's best we often think
and put self in the way,
God looks down and smiles at us
and says, such little faith.

He wants us to believe in Him
and trust His timely plan,
He then imparts to us great gifts
not always known to man.

So all we do is let it go
and give divine control,
the dreams we think beyond our reach
do manifest tenfold.

God within us give us strength
to live each day with joy,
as we pursue our purpose here
serving in love do employ.

With grateful hearts we thank you God
to us rich blessings give,
through all the lessons sent our way
you've shown us how to live.

And so it is…

—Carolyn Porter

CHAPTER 18

❧

A Celebrated Life

A celebrated life means living in a state of celebration. I picture this state of existence as fun, festive, exciting, dynamic, and wonderful. This life is about joy, not struggle. Each day is a gift and is lived to the fullest. Celebrating life produces positiveness. The glass is half-full, not half empty. The weather is partly sunny instead of partly cloudy. You have lessons and opportunities rather than problems and trials. It is a life of love, deep in the heart, that demonstrates faith, gratitude, appreciation, serving and great inner happiness.

Right now you might be thinking I have latched onto a Pollyanna viewpoint that is totally unrealistic. Who could ever be in a constant state of celebration in this day and age? It is possible and more people are experiencing this due to the awakening of what is really important in this life. In the next few paragraphs I'll share with you the qualities of the soul that characterize a life worth celebrating!

I believe that a celebrated life is a life of giving. As you reach out in love and touch someone you change lives, but most importantly, blessings come back and touch your heart. This is a life of service that involves sharing with others all that you have and all that you are. It always includes your purpose and, as you become your purpose and express it in living service, you are successful. Your work is love made visible. This is true happiness.

Real happiness always comes from within. Society tries to find happiness in a myriad ways, but it's only temporary because these things are external. A really happy person exudes a sparkle about being alive. This person jumps out of bed each morning excited that a new day is unfolding and anxious to see the miracles that day. When you find your purpose in life, which goes hand-in-hand with loving and serving, it literally transforms your existence. Both are so intertwined that they become part of you and are completely inseparable. There should be great joy in what you do; it should feed you and bring out your creativity and passion. It is at this point that you are genuinely fulfilled and happy.

A life of giving means just that—giving. There is never a thought of "I did that for him, so he should do this for me," which would be the expectation of returned favors. The beauty is that the ripples that come back far exceed what was put out there in the first place. People are often interested in what they get out of something. You might go to church to receive an inspiring message. You are involved in a relationship to be loved. You do a job for recognition or monetary reward. Instead, try changing your attitude of receiving into giving. Go to church and send love to all present. Give love to your partner without expecting anything in return. Do the best job you can because it needs to be done and you're happy to do it. This is the real attitude of giving.

Living a celebrated life is based on faith. Faith is the cornerstone in building a strong foundation for any purpose you pursue. God tells you to step out in faith when you know you should take a certain path. It may be well out of your comfort zone, but with God at the helm it's always the right direction. You will be guided in the work you are to complete. Your legs may wobble a

❦

bit, but the angels hold you firmly until you're steady on your feet once again.

Serving others with deepfelt caring puts sparkle in your eyes, a spring in your step and joy in your heart. Your love will pour out to others without even thinking about it; it'll be a natural expression of your inner happiness. It's a heart thing! This is enthusiasm. Enthus means God within us and it creates a desire in a person to move forward, demonstrating the energy of life moving through him. Two of the compliments I've received from people in recent months that have meant so much to me are the following: that I am bursting with enthusiasm and that I have passion for life. I now know that I am portraying what I feel inside and I thank God for showing me the way.

Gratitude is a vital aspect of living a celebrated life. No matter what state you are in or in what circumstance, you have much in which to be thankful. In fact, this is where you start by being thankful where you are. Then you thank God for all that He's bringing into your life. I personally begin every prayer by thanking God for a multitude of things. I write five items in my gratitude journal every night before bed and begin each day in an attitude of appreciation. A thankful heart is a loving heart. Every time a problem pops up I thank God because I'll be learning something new and therefore growing. Sometimes I thank Him through my tears. Being in a constant state of gratitude assures you of inner joy. So often people go on and on about all the trials and tribulations of life, but realize you are today a culmination of all that was before you. Thank God for it and be blessed by it because it made you who you are. It's pretty hard to wear a frown when you're authentically thankful.

Sow your seeds with love because you always reap what you sow. We are magnets, you and I, and attract into our lives what we radiate, because we are vibrational, energetic beings. The uni-

❧

verse is energy, so is all that is part of the universe. What you can conceive and believe you can achieve. It is in each thought we decide to keep that our life is created. Create the life you want rather than experiencing the life you have.

Our lives are to be dynamic, continually changing, as we upgrade daily. Each step we take puts us closer to our goal(s). It's a process which requires diligence and perseverance. Always focus on the outcome not the process. You can't climb from the basement to the second story in one or two steps, there are many to take along your journey. These steps of growth grow deeper as you experience all of your encounters. No matter what crosses your path you will be able to say, "and still I rise!" You will know you are on the correct path and God and your angels will guide you. It is then you sparkle with the elixir of life. Let your light shine brightly and illuminate the world.

You are now an empowered woman, one who is able to control the natural forces in life more effectively. You have a purpose and have fixed your eyes on your goal(s). With each step you take you gain more confidence that you will achieve your goals. You radiate inner happiness and serenity surrounds you. You know you are on the right path and your feet never waver. Fear is cast aside as you tackle difficult challenges, knowing you can meet those challenges with strength. You are a unique and magnificent individual with your own identity. As you access the spirit of life your greatness comes forth and you are liberated. Your spirit is flying free. You make a difference in this world. **You are a truly empowered woman!** *Carpe diem! Seize the day!*

STAR BRIGHT

Endings bring new beginnings—
One door closes, another opens and beckons to you.
Do not waver nor allow fear's illusions to overshadow you
For love surrounds you and angels guide you.
With each step you take, strengthening, growing,
Reaching for the heavens, beautifully empowered,
You are limitless!

Remember, a star shines in its own light.
Always live your dreams.
When darkness comes the beautiful star shines the brightest.
And so it is…

—CAROLYN PORTER

ENJOY YOUR JOURNEY DEAR FRIEND.

SUGGESTED READING

Truman, Karol K. "Feelings Buried Alive Never Die" Olympus Distributing, Las Vegas, Nevada 89193-7693, 1991

Williamson, Marianne "Enchanted Love" Simon & Schuster, New York, New York 10020, 2001

Jeffers, Susan, Ph.D. "End the Struggle and Dance With Life" St. Martin's Griffin, New York, New York 10010, 1997

Knight, John "Change Your Conversations...Change Your Life" Life is for Living, Inc., Atlanta, Georgia, 2001

Duckett, Dr. Michael J. "Breaking The Money Barriers" Whitmire Publishing, Marietta, Georgia 30066-0108, 1999

Beattie, Melody "Codependent No More" Hazelton, Center City, Minnesota 55012-0176, 1992

Williamson, Marianne "A Woman's Worth" Random House, Inc., New York, New York 10022, 1993

Hay, Louise L. "You Can Heal Your Life" Hay House, Inc., Carlsbad, California 92018-5100, 1999

Myss, Caroline, Ph.D. "Anatomy of the Spirit" Three Rivers Press, New York, New York 10022, 1996

Beathnach, Sarah Ban "Something More—Excavating Your Authentic Self" Warner Books, Inc., New York, New York 10020, 1998

Vanzant, Iyanla "In The Meantime" Simon & Schuster, New York, New York 10020, 1998

Beattie, Melody "Beyond Codependency" Harper & Row, San Francisco, California, 1989

Sullivan, Barbara "The Control Trap" Bethany House Publications, Minneapolis, Minnesota 55438, 1991

Dyer, Wayne "Real Magic" HarperCollins Publishers, New York, New York 10022, 1992

Williamson, Marianne "A Return To Love" HarperCollins Publishers, New York, New York 10022, 1992

Gray, Barbara "Success Through Spirituality for Women" Starlight Productions, Marietta, Georgia 30068, 1995

Gray, Barbara "Energy Management" Starlight Productions, Marietta, Georgia 30068, 2000